IMMM 2017

The Seventh International Conference on Advances in Information Mining and Management

DATASETS 2017

The International Symposium on Challenges for Designing and Using Datasets

June 25 - 29, 2017

Venice, Italy

IMMM 2017 Editors

Dirk Labudde, Hochschule Mittweida, Germany
Jaime Lloret Mauri, Polytechnic University of Valencia, Spain

Printed from e-media with permission by:

Curran Associates, Inc.
57 Morehouse Lane
Red Hook, NY 12571

Some format issues inherent in the e-media version may also appear in this print version.

Printed by Curran Associates, Inc. (2017)

International Academy, Research, and Industry Association (IARIA)
412 Derby Way
Wilmington, DE 19810

Phone: (408) 893-6407
Fax: (408) 527-6351

petre@iaria.org

Additional copies of this publication are available from:

Curran Associates, Inc.
57 Morehouse Lane
Red Hook, NY 12571 USA
Phone: 845-758-0400
Fax: 845-758-2633
Email: curran@proceedings.com
Web: www.proceedings.com

TABLE OF CONTENTS

IMMM 2017

Forward

The Seventh International Conference on Advances in Information Mining and Management (IMMM 2017), held between June 25-29, 2017 in Venice, Italy, continued a series of academic and industrial events focusing on advances in all aspects related to information mining, management, and use.

The amount of information and its complexity makes it difficult for our society to take advantage of the distributed knowledge value. Knowledge, text, speech, picture, data, opinion, and other forms of information representation, as well as the large spectrum of different potential sources (sensors, bio, geographic, health, etc.) led to the development of special mining techniques, mechanisms support, applications and enabling tools. However, the variety of information semantics, the dynamic of information update and the rapid change in user needs are challenging aspects when gathering and analyzing information.

The conference had the following tracks:

- Type of information mining
- Information mining and management
- Mining from specific sources
- Automated retrieval and mining

The conference included the following symposium:

- **DATASETS 2017**, The International Symposium on Designing, Validating, and Using Datasets

We take here the opportunity to warmly thank all the members of the IMMM 2017 technical program committee, as well as all the reviewers. The creation of such a high quality conference program would not have been possible without their involvement. We also kindly thank all the authors that dedicated much of their time and effort to contribute to IMMM 2017. We truly believe that, thanks to all these efforts, the final conference program consisted of top quality contributions.

We also gratefully thank the members of the IMMM 2017 organizing committee for their help in handling the logistics and for their work that made this professional meeting a success.

We hope that IMMM 2017 was a successful international forum for the exchange of ideas and results between academia and industry and to promote further progress in the area of information mining and management. We also hope that Venice, Italy provided a pleasant environment during the conference and everyone found some time to enjoy the unique charm of the city.

IMMM 2017 Chairs

IMMM Steering Committee
Nitin Agarwal, University of Arkansas at Little Rock, USA
Andreas Schmidt, Karlsruhe University of Applied Sciences, Germany
Michele Melchiori, Università degli Studi di Brescia, Italy
Bernhard Bauer, University of Augsburg, Germany
Mehmed Kantardzic, University of Louisville, USA
Daniel Thalmann, Institute for Media Innovation (IMI) | Nanyang Technological University, Singapore
Verena Kantere, University of Geneva, Switzerland
Duarte Trigueiros, ISCTE - University Institute of Lisbon, Portugal, Portugal

IMMM Industry/Research Advisory Committee
Dirk Labudde, Hochschule Mittweida, Germany
Adrienn Skrop, University of Pannonia, Hungary
Qing Liu, Data61 | CSIRO, Australia
Stefan Brüggemann, Airbus Defence and Space, Germany
Xuanwen Luo, Sandvik Mining, USA
Maria Luisa Villani, Italian National Agency for New Technologies, Energy and Sustainable Economic Development (ENEA), Italy
Emir Muñoz, Fujitsu Ireland Ltd / INSIGHT Centre at NUI Galway, Ireland
Xiang Ji, Bloomberg LP, USA

DATASETS 2017 Chairs

DATASETS Advisory Committee
Yun-Maw Kevin Cheng [鄭穎懋], Tatung University Taipei, Taiwan
Sebastian Maneth, University of Edinburgh, UK
Verena Kantere, University of Geneva, Switzerland
Mariana Damova, Mozajka Ltd., Bulgaria

IMMM 2017
Committee

IMMM Steering Committee

Nitin Agarwal, University of Arkansas at Little Rock, USA
Andreas Schmidt, Karlsruhe University of Applied Sciences, Germany
Michele Melchiori, Università degli Studi di Brescia, Italy
Bernhard Bauer, University of Augsburg, Germany
Mehmed Kantardzic, University of Louisville, USA
Daniel Thalmann, Institute for Media Innovation (IMI) | Nanyang Technological University, Singapore
Verena Kantere, University of Geneva, Switzerland
Duarte Trigueiros, ISCTE - University Institute of Lisbon, Portugal, Portugal

IMMM Industry/Research Advisory Committee

Dirk Labudde, Hochschule Mittweida, Germany
Adrienn Skrop, University of Pannonia, Hungary
Qing Liu, Data61 | CSIRO, Australia
Stefan Brüggemann, Airbus Defence and Space, Germany
Xuanwen Luo, Sandvik Mining, USA
Maria Luisa Villani, Italian National Agency for New Technologies, Energy and Sustainable Economic Development (ENEA), Italy
Emir Muñoz, Fujitsu Ireland Ltd / INSIGHT Centre at NUI Galway, Ireland
Xiang Ji, Bloomberg LP, USA

IMMM 2017 Technical Program Committee

Nitin Agarwal, University of Arkansas at Little Rock, USA
Zaher Al Aghbari, University of Sharjah, UAE
Liliana Ibeth Barbosa-Santillan, University of Guadalajara, Mexico
Cristina Barros, University of Alicante, Spain
Bernhard Bauer, University of Augsburg, Germany
Stefan Brüggemann, Airbus Defence and Space, Germany
Erik Cambria, Nanyang Technological University, Singapore
Mirko Cesarini, University of Milan Bicocca, Italy
Nadezda Chalupova, Mendel University in Brno, Czech Republic
Pascal Cuxac, INIST-CNRS, Nancy, France
Mirela Danubianu, "Stefan cel Mare" University of Suceava, Romania
František Dařena, Mendel University Brno, Czech Republic
Ke Deng, RMIT University, Melbourne, Australia
Qin Ding, East Carolina University, USA

Daniel Garijo, Universidad Politénica de Madrid, Spain
Paolo Garza, Politecnico di Torino, Italy
Ilias Gialampoukidis, Centre for Research and Technology Hellas | Information Technologies Institute, Thessaloniki, Greece
Alessandro Giuliani, University of Cagliari, Italy
William Grosky, University of Michigan-Dearborn, USA
Soumaya Guesmi, LIPAH | Université de Tunis El Manar, Tunisia
Fikret Gurgen, Bogazici University, Turkey
Shakhmametova Gyuzel, Ufa State Aviation Technical University, Russia
Tzung-Pei Hong, National University of Kaohsiung, Taiwan
Yin-Fu Huang, National Yunlin University of Science and Technology, Taiwan
Sergio Ilarri, University of Zaragoza, Spain
Xiang Ji, Bloomberg LP, USA
Konstantinos Kalpakis, University of Maryland Baltimore County, USA
Mehmed Kantardzic, University of Louisville, USA
Verena Kantere, University of Geneva, Switzerland
Sokratis K. Katsikas, Center for Cyber & Information Security | Norwegian University of Science & Technology (NTNU), Norway
Young-Gab Kim, Sejong University, South Korea
Piotr Kulczycki, Systems Research Institute | Polish Academy of Sciences, Poland
Dirk Labudde, Hochschule Mittweida, Germany
Cristian Lai, ISOC - Information SOCiety | CRS4 - Center for Advanced Studies, Research and Development in Sardinia, Italy
Mariusz Łapczyński, Cracow University of Economics, Poland
Georgios Lappas, Western Macedonia University of Applied Sciences, Greece
Anne Laurent, University of Montpellier, France
Kang Li, Groupon Inc., USA
Dimitrios Liparas, Information Technologies Institute | Centre for Research and Technology Hellas, Greece
Qing Liu, Data61 | CSIRO, Australia
Elena Lloret, University of Alicante, Spain
Flaminia Luccio, Università Ca' Foscari Venezia, Italy
Xuanwen Luo, Sandvik Mining, USA
Stephane Maag, Telecom SudParis, France
Francesco Marcelloni, University of Pisa, Italy
Subhasish Mazumdar, New Mexico Tech (New Mexico Institute of Mining and Technology), USA
Michele Melchiori, Università degli Studi di Brescia, Italy
Fabio Mercorio, University of Milano – Bicocca, Italy
José Manuel Molina López, Universidad Carlos III de Madrid, Spain
Emir Muñoz, Fujitsu Ireland Ltd / INSIGHT Centre at NUI Galway, Ireland
Pernelle Nathalie, LRI - University Paris Sud, France
Erich Neuhold, University of Vienna, Austria
Jose R. Parama, Universidade da Coruña, Spain
Hai Phan, Ying Wu College of Computing | New Jersey Institute of Technology, USA

Ioannis Pratikakis, Democritus University of Thrace, Xanthi, Greece
Lorenza Saitta, Università del Piemonte Orientale, Italy
Andreas Schmidt, Karlsruhe Institute of Technology / University of Applied Sciences Karlsruhe, Germany
Josep Silva, Universitat Politècnica de València, Spain
Adrienn Skrop, University of Pannonia, Hungary
Dora Souliou, National Technical University of Athens, Greece
Armando Stellato, University of Rome Tor Vergata, Italy
Alvaro Suarez, Las Palmas de Gran Canaria University, Spain
Tatiana Tambouratzis, University of Piraeus, Greece
Abdullah Abdullah Uz Tansel, Baruch College CUNY, USA
Daniel Thalmann, Institute for Media Innovation (IMI) | Nanyang Technological University, Singapore
Valeria Times, Center for Informatics - Federal University of Pernambuco (CIn/UFPE), Brazil
Duarte Trigueiros, ISCTE - University Institute of Lisbon, Portugal, Portugal
Chrisa Tsinaraki, European Union - Joint Research Center (JRC), Italy
Lorna Uden, Staffordshire University, UK
Marta Vicente, University of Alicante, Spain
Maria Luisa Villani, Italian National Agency for New Technologies, Energy and Sustainable Economic Development (ENEA), Italy
Stefanos Vrochidis, Information Technologies Institute - Centre for Research and Technology Hellas, Greece
Hao Wu, Yunnan University, China

DATASETS 2017

DATASETS Advisory Committee

Yun-Maw Kevin Cheng [鄭穎懋], Tatung University Taipei, Taiwan
Sebastian Maneth, University of Edinburgh, UK
Verena Kantere, University of Geneva, Switzerland
Mariana Damova, Mozajka Ltd., Bulgaria

DATASETS 2017 Program Committee Members

Patrick Appiah-Kubi, University of Maryland University College, USA
Yun-Maw Kevin Cheng, Tatung University Taipei, Taiwan
Mariana Damova, Mozajka Ltd., Bulgaria
Ana García-Serrano, ETSI Informática - UNED, Madrid, Spain
Verena Kantere, University of Geneva, Switzerland
Sebastian Maneth, University of Edinburgh, UK
Armando Stellato, University of Rome Tor Vergata, Italy
Alvaro Suarez, Las Palmas de Gran Canaria University, Spain

Copyright Information

A Parallelized Learning Algorithm for Monotonicity Constrained Support Vector Machines

Hui-Chi Chuang
Institute of Information Management
National Cheng Kung University
Tainan City, Taiwan, R.O.C.
e-mail: huichi613@gmail.com

Chih-Chuan Chen
Interdisciplinary Program of Green and Information Technology
National Taitung University
Taitung, Taiwan, R.O.C.
e-mail: ccchen@nttu.edu.tw

Chi Chou
Institute of Information Management
National Cheng Kung University
Tainan City, Taiwan, R.O.C.
e-mail: cycle-zz@hotmail.com

Yi-Chung Cheng
Department of International Business Management
Tainan University of Technology
Tainan City, Taiwan, R.O.C.
e-mail: t20042@mail.tut.edu.tw

Sheng-Tun Li
Institute of Information Management, Department of Industrial and Information Management
National Cheng Kung University
Tainan City, Taiwan, R.O.C.
e-mail: stli@mail.ncku.edu.tw

***Abstract*—Various efforts have been made to improve support vector machines (SVMs) based on different scenarios of real world problems. SVMs are the so-called benchmarking neural network technology motivated by the results of statistical learning theory. Among them, taking into account experts' knowledge has been confirmed to help SVMs deal with noisy data to obtain more useful results. For example, SVMs with monotonicity constraints and with the Tikhonov regularization method, also known as Regularized Monotonic SVM (RMC-SVM) incorporate inequality constraints into SVMs based on the monotonic property of real-world problems, and the Tikhonov regularization method is further applied to ensure that the solution is unique and bounded. These kinds of SVMs are also referred to as knowledge-oriented SVMs. However, solving SVMs with monotonicity constraints will require even more computation than SVMs. In this research, a parallelized learning strategy is proposed to solve the regularized monotonicity constrained SVMs. Due to the characteristics of the parallelized learning method, the dataset can be divided into several parts for parallel computing at different times. This study proposes a RMC-SVMs with a parallel strategy to reduce the required training time and to increase the feasibility of using RMC-SVMs in real world applications.**

Keywords-support vector machines; monotonic prior knowledge; learning algorithm; parallel strategy

I. INTRODUCTION

It is well-known that we are currently in the Big Data and Internet of Things (IOT) era. The progress in data processing and analyzing ability of computer hardware has fallen behind the growth of information such that the datasets are becoming too large to handle on a single hardware unit. In response, in this study we introduce an algorithm to deal with large-scale data by using a parallel strategy.

Many advanced data mining methods are being rapidly developed. Support Vector Machines (SVMs), were pioneered by Vapnik in 1995, and constitute a state-of-the-art artificial neural network (ANN) based on statistical learning [1], [2]. SVMs have been widely applied in many fields over the past few years, such as corporate distress, consumer loan evaluation, text categorization, handwritten digit recognition, speaker verification and many others.

Knowledge engineering is a process of developing an expert system that utilizes stored knowledge to achieve a higher performance, especially focusing on the knowledge provided by human experts in a specific field; in contrast, data mining focuses on data available in an organization. Recently, Li and Chen proposed a regularized monotonic SVM (RMC-SVM) for classification to a broader aspect of SVM by incorporating domain related intelligence in support vector learners for mining actionable knowledge for real-world applications [3], [4].

SVMs have high computing-time costs during the training procedure. The time complexity of SVMs is $O(n^2m)$ where m represents the number of attributes and n represents the amount of data. So, if the data scale increases, SVM training becomes more complex and so requires more computational time. In addition, the SVMs model with regularized monotonic (RMC-SVM) causes change the structure of quadratic programming problem of SVMs and time complexity is more complicated. However, traditional training algorithms for SVMs, such as chunking and sequential minimal optimization (SMO) [5], [6], have computation complexity dependent on the amount of data, and become infeasible when dealing with large scale problems [7] and SVMs with monotonicity constraints. We chose the numerical analysis method with parallel strategy to solve the aforementioned problems.

The learning algorithm, proposed by Hestenes and Stiefel (1952), is an efficient numerical analysis method that converges quickly to find optimal solutions. With the characteristic of the parallelized learning algorithm, the dataset can be easily divided into P parts for parallel computing at different times or in separate computer hardware units. The parallelized learning algorithm is highly efficient in solving RMC- SVM and enhances the RMC-SVM algorithm making it more practical to use.

II. LITERATURE REVIEW

This section provides a review of the Support Vector Machines and the related literature to build the foundation of our study.

SVMs are the so-called benchmarking neural network technology motivated by the results of statistical learning theory [2], [8]. SVMs are primarily designed for binary classification, attempting to find out the optimal hyper-plane that separates the negative datasets from the positive datasets with maximum margin. They were originally developed for pattern recognition [9], and used a typically small subset of all training examples called the support vector to represent the decision boundary [10]. The optimal hyper-plane will accurately separate the data if the problem is linearly separable. However, since most of the datasets are non-separable, SVMs first map the same points onto a high-dimensional feature space to successfully separate non-separable data by the linear decision boundary in the input space. Moreover, SVMs use inner-product to overcome the high-dimensionality problems that machine learning methods are too difficult to solve [11].

For the purpose of improving the effectiveness or efficiency of SVMs, several theoretical studies have been conducted to modify or reformulate the conventional SVM model. Kramer et al. [12] presented a fast compression method to scale up SVMs to handle large datasets by applying a simple bit-reduction method to reduce the cardinality of the data by weighting representative examples. Also, Yu et al. [13] proposed two implementations of the block minimization framework for primal and dual SVMs, and then analyzed the framework for data which is larger than the memory size. At each step, a block of data is loaded from the disk and handled by certain learning methods. In recent years, the applications of SVM methods still exist over a wide range of fields.

Monotonicity is considered as a common form of prior knowledge and it can be constructed by lots of properties. Practically, people hope that the predictor variable and responding variable can satisfy the monotonicity property in problems. Pazzani et al. [14] addressed the importance of using monotonicity constraints in classification problems. Doumpos and Zopounidis [15] proposed a monotonic support vector machine. The virtual examples in this approach are generated from using the monotonicity "hints" to impose monotonic conditions, which represent prior knowledge associated with the problem. Finally, the model can reach a higher prediction accuracy and have a better prediction ability. Li and Chen [4] formulated a knowledge-oriented classification model by directly adding monotonicity constraints into the optimization model. To ensure the solution is unique and bounded, they applied Tikhonov regularization to alleviate the predicament caused by adding monotonicity constraints that might lead to the loss of convexity [16], [17]. With the above study, we find that prior knowledge can increase the accuracy and bring up more valuable knowledge from data. We construct a SVM with monotonicity constraints and improve the result of the classification problem.

The learning method is one of the most useful techniques for solving large linear systems of equations, and it can also be adapted to solve nonlinear optimization problems. Besides, it is an iterative way to solve linear systems or nonlinear optimization problems and was introduced by Hestenes and Stiefel [18]. Thus, we can see that the parallelized learning method is very well suited for solving large problems.

The LS-SVM is an iterative training algorithm which is based on the parallelized learning method [19]. Moreover, the parallelized learning with SVMs is also used for intrusion detection [20]. Recently, Kaytez et al. [21] used LS-SVM to forecast the electricity consumption.

In many practical SVM applications, standard quadratic programming (QP) solvers based on the explicit storage of the Hessian matrix G may be very inefficient or even inapplicable due to excessive memory requirements. When facing large scale problems, exploiting the inherent parallelism of data mining algorithms provides a direct solution by using the large data retrieval and processing power of parallel architectures. On parallelization of SVM, several issues must be addressed to achieve good performance, such as limiting the overhead for kernel evaluations and choosing a suitable inner QP solver. Zanghirati and Zanni [22] obtained an efficient sub-problem solution by a gradient projection-type method, which exploits the simple structure of the constraints, exhibits good convergence rate and is well suited for a parallel implementation. Other parallel approaches to SVMs have been proposed, by splitting the training data into subsets and distributing them to processors [23], [24]. Zani et al. [25] implemented a parallel software for solving the quadratic programming arising in training SVMs for classification.

III. RESEARCH METHODOLOGY

Let N be the data number, and n be the number of attributes. A dataset $\mathfrak{J} = \{(x_i, y_i) \mid i = 1,2,\dots,\mathrm{N}\}$, with input data $x_i \in \mathcal{R}^n$ and output data $y_i \in \mathcal{R}$. Then, the function $\mathcal{F}(x) : \mathcal{R}^n \to \mathcal{R}$ is to stand for using input variables to classify the output variable. A partial ordering $\leq$ is defined over input space $\mathcal{R}^n$. A linear ordering $\leq$ is defined over the space $\mathcal{R}$ with class labels as integer values y_i. The classified function is monotonic if it satisfies the following statement:

$$x_i \leq x_j \Rightarrow \mathcal{F}(x_i) \leq \mathcal{F}(x_j), \quad \text{for any } x_i \text{ and } x_j \quad (1)$$

In this paper, we define the partial order on the input space $\mathcal{R}^n$ in an intuitive way such that for $x = (x_1, x_2, \dots, x_n)$ and $x' = (x'_1, x'_2, \dots, x'_n)$, we say $x \leq x'$ if and only if $x \leq x'$ for $i = 1,2,\dots,\mathrm{n}$. For a classification problem, we say a target function has a monotonicity property if the experts perceive it as monotonic.

This study adopted a heuristic approach to enhance the monotonicity of an SVM classifier. To incorporate the monotonic prior knowledge into a problem, we denote a number of random pairs of virtual examples as

$$MC = \{(\underline{x}_k, \overline{x}_k) | \text{for all observed } \underline{x}_k \leq \overline{x}_k, k = 1, \dots, M\}.$$

The predicted outcomes of the SVM classifier should satisfy the monotonicity constraints, $\mathcal{F}(x_i) \leq \mathcal{F}(x_j)$ for $k = 1, \dots, M$, as closely as possible.

The idea of creating monotonicity constraints is straightforward since this kind of prior knowledge is provided by human experts from a specific field. Due to the expectation that the respective predicted classes y and y' satisfy the condition $y \leq y'$, constraints $\boldsymbol{w}^T\boldsymbol{\varphi}(\boldsymbol{x}) \leq \boldsymbol{w}^T\boldsymbol{\varphi}(\boldsymbol{x}')$ can be added into a model for each pair of input vectors $\boldsymbol{x} \leq \boldsymbol{x}'$ to hold the monotonicity.

The primal SVM model is presented as

$$\begin{aligned} \min \quad & J(\boldsymbol{w}, \boldsymbol{\varepsilon}) = \frac{1}{2}\|\boldsymbol{w}\|^2 + C\sum_{i=1}^{N} \varepsilon_i, \\ \textit{subject to} \quad & y_i(\boldsymbol{w}^T\boldsymbol{\varphi}(x_i) + b) \geq 1 - \varepsilon_i, \ i = 1, \dots, N, \\ & \varepsilon_i \geq 0, i = 1, \dots, N \end{aligned} \quad (2)$$

From the previous section, we know how monotonicity constraints can be constructed; and here, they are expressed as the following inequality:

$$\boldsymbol{w}^T\boldsymbol{\varphi}(\underline{\boldsymbol{x}}) \leq \boldsymbol{w}^T\boldsymbol{\varphi}(\overline{\boldsymbol{x}}), \text{for observation } \underline{\boldsymbol{x}} \leq \overline{\boldsymbol{x}}. \quad (3)$$

By adding the monotonicity constraints to SVM, the model becomes as shown below and it is called MCSVM.

$$\begin{aligned} \min \quad & J(\boldsymbol{w}, \boldsymbol{\varepsilon}) = \frac{1}{2}\|\boldsymbol{w}\|^2 + C\sum_{i=1}^{N} \varepsilon_i, \\ \textit{subject to} \quad & y_i(\boldsymbol{w}^T\boldsymbol{\varphi}(x_i) + b) \geq 1 - \varepsilon_i, \ i = 1, \dots, N, \\ & \boldsymbol{w}^T\boldsymbol{\varphi}(\underline{\boldsymbol{x}}_k) \leq \boldsymbol{w}^T\boldsymbol{\varphi}(\overline{\boldsymbol{x}}_k), \text{for observations} \\ & \underline{\boldsymbol{x}}_k \leq \overline{\boldsymbol{x}}_k, k = 1, \dots, M, \\ & \varepsilon_i \geq 0, i = 1, \dots, N. \end{aligned} \quad (4)$$

Note that both the objective function and constraints are nonlinear in the above optimization problem. Since it is quite complicated to directly solve the problem in (5) with the possibility of $\boldsymbol{\varphi}(\boldsymbol{x})$ and $\boldsymbol{w}$ being infinite dimensional, this problem can be solved in the dual space of a Lagrangian multiplier. When the kernel does not satisfy Mercer's condition, it is possible that the matrix G is indefinite depending on the training data, and in this case the quadratic programming is non-convex and may have no solution [11]. Accordingly, the well-known Tikhonov regularization approach is applied to avoid this situation [16], [17]. A penalty term, δ which is set to be two times the absolute value of the minimal negative eigenvalue of matrix G is added to the objective function, after which the regularized model becomes

$$\begin{aligned} \min_{\boldsymbol{\alpha},\boldsymbol{\beta}} \tilde{Q}(\boldsymbol{\alpha}, \boldsymbol{\beta}) &= \frac{1}{2}[\boldsymbol{\alpha}^T \quad \boldsymbol{\beta}^T](\mathrm{G} + \delta\mathbf{I})\begin{bmatrix}\boldsymbol{\alpha}\\ \boldsymbol{\beta}\end{bmatrix} - 1^T\boldsymbol{\alpha}, \\ \textit{Subject to} \quad & \sum_{i=1}^{N} \alpha_i y_i = 0, \\ & 0 \leq \alpha_i \leq C, i = 1, \dots, N, \\ & \beta_k \geq 0, \forall k = 1, \dots, M. \end{aligned} \quad (5)$$

where **I** is the identity matrix. With an appropriate choice of δ, the quadratic programming problem would be convex and have a global solution. The resulting model is called a Regularized Monotonic SVM (RMC-SVM) model.

Finally, with an appropriate choice of kernel K, the nonlinear RMC-SVM classifier takes the form:

$$y(\boldsymbol{x}) = sign\left[\sum_{i=1}^{N} \alpha_i y_i K(x_i, \boldsymbol{x}) + \sum_{k=1}^{M} \beta_k \left(K(\overline{x}_k, \boldsymbol{x}) - K(\underline{x}_k, \boldsymbol{x})\right) + b\right] \quad (6)$$

where the $K(\boldsymbol{x}_i, \boldsymbol{x}_j) = \boldsymbol{\varphi}(\boldsymbol{x}_i)^T\boldsymbol{\varphi}(\boldsymbol{x}_j)$

The solutions, $\alpha_i's$ and $\beta_k's$, are derived from the quadratic programming problem in (6).

The parallelized learning method, introduced by Hestenes and Stiefel [18], is an iterative method and one of the most useful techniques for solving large linear systems of equations; additionally, it can also be adapted to solve nonlinear optimization problems. The Parallelized learning method proceeds by generating vector sequences of iterates, residuals corresponding to iterates, and search directions used in updating iterates and residuals. In every iteration of the method, two inner products are performed in order to compute update scalars that are defined to ensure the vector sequences satisfy certain orthogonality conditions. On a symmetric positive definite linear system, these conditions imply that the distance to the true solution is minimized in some norm.

We take the parallelized learning method to solve the RMC-SVM model which is one of the numerical analysis methods used in this paper. The original RMC-SVM model is a quadratic programming problem with the constraints, including the equality constraint and the box constraint.

The box constraint restricts the range of estimate solutions, which has upper and lower bounds. Due to the parallelized learning method being used to solve unconstrained optimization problems, we modified it. We used the Lagrangian multiplier to transform the equality constraint into an objective function. Furthermore, we restrict the upper and the lower bounds of the estimate solution to deal with the box constraint in each iteration. We use the Lagrangian multiplier to transform equality constraint into an objective function.

$$\begin{aligned} \tilde{\mathcal{L}}(\boldsymbol{\alpha}, \boldsymbol{\beta}, \boldsymbol{\lambda}) &= \frac{1}{2}[\boldsymbol{\alpha}^T \quad \boldsymbol{\beta}^T](\mathrm{G} + \delta\mathbf{I})\begin{bmatrix}\boldsymbol{\alpha}\\ \boldsymbol{\beta}\end{bmatrix} - e^T\boldsymbol{\alpha} + \boldsymbol{\lambda}^T(\boldsymbol{\alpha}y) \\ &= \frac{1}{2}[\boldsymbol{\alpha}^T \quad \boldsymbol{\beta}^T](\mathrm{G} + \delta\mathbf{I})\begin{bmatrix}\boldsymbol{\alpha}\\ \boldsymbol{\beta}\end{bmatrix} - (e^T - \boldsymbol{\lambda}^T y)\,\boldsymbol{\alpha} \end{aligned} \quad (7)$$

The details of parallelized learning method to solve the RMC-SVM are shown in Figure 1.

> Let the objective function $F(x) = \frac{1}{2}x^TQx - e^Tx$ where x is an n by n matrix with the equality constraint $G(x) = yx$
> Initiate vector, including the number of executions, the estimate solution, and search direction
> Repeat
> 1. Compute the scalar α and update the next estimate solution
> 2. Compute the Lagrangian multiplier λ and $\nabla L(x) = \nabla F(x) + \lambda\,\nabla G(x)$
> 3. Update the search direction $d^{(k+1)} = \nabla L(x) + r^k d^{(k)}$ where $r^k = \frac{\nabla L(x^{k+1}) * \nabla L(x^{k+1})^T}{\nabla L(x^k) * \nabla L(x^k)^T}$
>
> Until (the number of executions <= n or residual error < ε)

Figure 1. Process of parallelized learning method to solve the RMC-SVM

Due to the structure of the SVM model with monotonicity constraints, the model becomes increasingly complicated. As such, we take the parallel strategy to solve the complex RMC-SVM model. It is similar to the Divide-and-Conquer algorithm. First, the dataset is averagely divided into m parts, which is called divide. Second, each part of the dataset is individually operated, which is called conquer. Finally, the mixture algorithm is used to integrate the results of different parts. To parallelize RMC-SVM, we first split the dataset and apply the parallelized learning algorithm proposed in the previous subsection. For data splitting, the parallel mixture of SVMs for large scale problems [23] is adopted for solving RMC-SVM. The idea is to divide the training set into m random subsets of approximately equal size. Each subset, called an expert, is then trained separately and the optimal solutions of all sub- SVMs are combined into a weighted sum, called "gater" module, to create a mixture of SVMs.

Finally, another optimization process is applied to determine the optimal mixture. The idea of mixtures has given rise to very popular SVM training algorithms.

The output of the mixture is defined as follow

$$f(x) = [h \sum_{j=1}^{P} \omega_j(x) S_j(x)] \quad (8)$$

where h is a transfer function which could be, for instance, the hyperbolic tangent for classification tasks. $\omega_i\ (x)$ is the gater weight, and is trained to minimize the cost function:

$$\omega = \sum_{i=1}^{N} [f(x_i) - y_i\ ] \quad (9)$$

$S_i(x)$ is the output of each expert, and the output in RMC-SVM is as follows:

$$S_i(x) = \sum_{i=1}^{N} \alpha_i y_i K(x_i, x) + \sum_{k=1}^{M} \beta_k \left(K(\overline{x}_k, x) - K(\underline{x}_k, x)\right) + b \quad (10)$$

IV. EXPERIMENTAL RESULTS AND ANALYSIS

We evaluate the performance of the proposed parallel strategy algorithm to solve the RMC-SVM problem and discuss comparisons of the prediction results obtained by RMC-SVM, Mixture SVM and Mixture RMC-SVM on three real-world datasets.

Due to the dataset being too large for us to handle at one time, in this research we propose a more efficient algorithm that can accelerate the training time. In the experiment, we used three real-world datasets as presented in next subsection, the codes of which are executed in MATLAB R2015a on an Intel Core i7-4770 CPU 3.2 GHz with 16 GB RAM running Window Server 2008. Additionally, we use the same RBF kernel function with different methods.

In the experiment, we have nine steps, for which the details are listed as follows.

Step1. Preprocess the data and normalize each data element in the dataset.

Step2. Randomly partition the dataset into a two-one-split training set and a testing set.

Step3. In the same partitioned dataset, respectively train the data with RMC-SVM Mixture SVM and Mixture RMC-SVM.

Step4. In the Mixture RMC-SVM, divide the training set into *m* parts, and each part respectively constructs monotonic constraints.

Step5. For each part use grid search to find the optimal parameters C and σ.

$C = \{0.01\ 0.05\ 0.1\ 0.5\ 1\ 5\ 10\ 50\ 100\ 500\ 1000\}$,
$\sigma = \{0.5\ 5\ 10\ 15\ 25\ 50\ 100\ 250\ 500\}$.

Step6. Use the output of each part to calculate the gater weight.

Step7. Compute the parameter mixture to integrate the output from each part and classify the data of the testing data.

Step8. Repeat step2 to step7 for 30 times.

Step9. Analyze the average performance result of the 30 times.

Our research conducted the experiments with one real-world dataset from the UCI [26] machine learning repository: Wisconsin Diagnostic Breast Cancer (WDBC). The WDBC dataset is computed from digitized images of fine needle-aspirated (FNA) breast mass, in which characteristics of the cell nuclei present in the images are described. For the WDBC dataset, there were 683 instances after removing missing values. Furthermore, each instance consists of nine attributes and distinguishes the class label for whether the cell is malignant or benign.

In this research, we compare our proposed parallel strategy algorithm with MCSVM. The performance results are examined in terms of Accuracy, F-measure, frequency monotonicity rate (FMR) and training time.

Accuracy is the most intuitive measurement criterion, which directly defines the predictive ability based on the proportion of the tested data that are correctly classified, and is defined as follows:

$$Accuracy = \frac{TP + TN}{TP + FP + TN + FN} \quad (11)$$

Recall, also called Sensitivity, measures the proportion of actual positives that are correctly identified as such, and is defined as follows:

$$Recall = \frac{TP}{TP + FN} \quad (12)$$

The precision rate, also named Positive Predictive Value (PPV), is the proportion of test instances with positive predictive outcomes that are correctly predicted. It is the most important measure of a predictive method, as it reflects the probability that a positive test reflects the underlying condition being tested for. It is defined as:

$$Precision = \frac{TP}{TP + FP} \quad (13)$$

The traditional F-measure is the harmonic mean of recall (Sensitivity) and precision (PPV), and is defined as:

$$F - measure = 2 \cdot \frac{PPV \cdot Sensitivity}{PPV + Sensitivity} \quad (14)$$

The F-measure takes both recall and precision into account, thereby avoiding a situation with low recall and high precision, or vice versa.

We use the Frequency Monotonicity Rate (FMR) to measure the monotonicity of the dataset $\mathfrak{I} = \{(x_i, y_i) | i = 1,2, \ldots, N\}$, which is defined as the proportion of data pairs in a dataset that do not violate the monotonicity condition. It is defined as:

$$FMR = \frac{FM}{P} = \frac{\text{Number}((x_i \geq x_j) \wedge (y_i \geq y_j))}{C_2^N} \quad (15)$$

where P is the number of observed pairs, and FM is the number of pairs that do not violate the monotonicity condition. Note that the monotonicity measure FMR can also be applied to a classifier in order to measure its capability of retaining monotonicity in an unseen dataset.

In the experiment, we conducted each process in the same training dataset. Both RMC-SVM and Mixture RMC-SVM used the hierarchy method to construct monotonicity constraints. It should be noted that the experiments carried out in this research have the following two different numbers of constraints:

number of constraints={63,127}

In this paper, we use the parallel strategy to solve the quadratic programming problem of RMC-SVM. We have two diverse directions to construct monotonicity constraints. We can use the whole training dataset or the dataset that divides the whole training dataset into different parts to construct monotonicity constraints. In the parallel strategy, the dataset is divided into different parts. Thus, the experiments selected three different numbers of parts to divide the whole dataset:

number of parts={2,4,6}

TABLE I. WDBC DATASET RESULTS

Monotonicity Constraints	Classifier	Accuracy	F-measure	FMR	Time(s)
63	RMC-SVM	0.95800	0.94142	0.99987	61.7736
	RMC-MIX 2 Part	0.96696	0.95371	1	14.4704
	RMC-MIX 4 Part	0.96461	0.95063	1	11.6556
	RMC-MIX 6 Part	0.96197	0.94761	1	12.0382
127	RMC-SVM	0.95888	0.94271	0.99988	79.2382
	RMC-MIX 2 Part	0.96784	0.95466	1	22.7641
	RMC-MIX 4 Part	0.96505	0.95133	1	21.0593
	RMC-MIX 6 Part	0.96652	0.95347	1	24.8682

V. CONCLUSIONS AND SUGGESTIONS

In this paper, parallel strategy was used to solve SVMs with monotonicity constraints (RMC-SVM) in which the whole training dataset was partitioned into smaller subsets and then RMC-SVM was parallelly applied to each of the partitioned subsets. Furthermore, a mixture method was used to integrate the results from all subsets and to classify the testing dataset. Our experiment on two real world datasets demonstrated the efficiency of the parallel strategy RMC-SVM.

We explored the efficiency of the predictive performance of the parallel strategy to solve RMC-SVM with different numbers of parts to divide the whole training dataset in, as well as diverse directions to construct the monotonicity constraints. The experiment showed that the efficiency of the parallel strategy RMC-SVM decreases as the number of parts increases. It is because there is more communication and integration time with the use of more parts. Moreover, most of the experimental results showed that the proposed method had a better performance if the whole training dataset was used to construct monotonicity constraints as compared with using the subsets to construct monotonicity constraints. In the further, we will implement more experiments to verify our method.

ACKNOWLEDGMENT

This research was supported in part by the Ministry of Science and Technology, ROC, under contract MOST 105-2410-H-006-038-MY3. The authors also thank Mr. Chi Chou for his help on the experimentation.

REFERENCES

[1] Vapnik, "The Nature of Statistical Learning Theory," 1995.

[2] V. Vapnik, "Statistical learning theory," Wiley: New York,Vol. 1, 1998.

[3] C. C. Chen, and S. T. Li, "Credit rating with a monotonicity-constrained support vector machine model. Expert Systems with Applications," Vol. 41(16), 7235-7247, 2014.

[4] S. T. Li, and C. C. Chen, "A regularized monotonic fuzzy support vector machine model for data mining with prior knowledge," IEEE Transactions on Fuzzy Systems, vol. 23(5), 1713-1727, 2015.

[5] C. C. Chang, and C. J. Lin, "LIBSVM: a library for support vector machines," ACM Transactions on Intelligent Systems and Technology (TIST), vol. 2(3), 27, 2011.

[6] C. J. Platt, "12 fast training of support vector machines using sequential minimal optimization," Advances in kernel methods, 185-208, 1999.

[7] A. K. Menon, "Large-scale support vector machines: algorithms and theory," Research Exam, University of California, San Diego, 1-17, 2009.

[8] C. Cortes, and V. Vapnik, "Support-vector networks," Machine learning, vol. 20(3), 273-297, 1995.

[9] B. E. Boser, I. M. Guyon, and V. N. Vapnik, "A training algorithm for optimal margin classifiers," Paper presented at the Proceedings of the fifth annual workshop on Computational learning theory, 1992.

[10] B. SchiilkopP, C. Burgest, and V. Vapnik, "Extracting support data for a given task." no. x, 1995.

[11] C. J. Burges, "A tutorial on support vector machines for pattern recognition," Data mining and knowledge discovery, vol. 2(2), 121-167, 1998.

[12] K. Kramer, L. O. Hall, D. B. Goldgof, A. Remsen, and T. Luo, "Fast support vector machines for continuous data," Systems, Man, and Cybernetics, Part B: Cybernetics, IEEE Transactions on, vol. 39(4), 989-1001, 2009.

[13] H. F. Yu, C. J. Hsieh, K. W. Chang, and C. J. Lin, "Large linear classification when data cannot fit in memory," ACM Transactions on Knowledge Discovery from Data (TKDD), vol. 5(4), 23, 2012.

[14] M. J. Pazzani, S. Mani, and W. R. Shankle, "Acceptance of rules generated by machine learning among medical experts," Methods of information in medicine, vol. 40(5), 380-385, 2001.

[15] M. Doumpos, and C. Zopounidis, "Monotonic support vector machines for credit risk rating," New Mathematics and Natural Computation, vol. 5(3), 557-570, 2009.

[16] C. M. Maes, "A regularized active-set method for sparse convex quadratic programming," Citeseer, 2010.

[17] A. N. Tikhonov, and V. I. A. k. Arsenin, "Solutions of ill-posed problems: Vh Winston," 1977.

[18] M. R. Hestenes, and E. Stiefel, "Methods of learnings for solving linear systems," 1952.

[19] J. Suykens, L. Lukas, P. Van Dooren, B. De Moor, and J. Vandewalle, "Least squares support vector machine classifiers: a large scale algorithm," Paper presented at the European Conference on Circuit Theory and Design, ECCTD, 1999.

[20] S. Mukkamala, G. Janoski, and A. Sung, "Intrusion detection using neural networks and support vector machines," Paper presented at the Neural Networks, 2002. IJCNN'02. Proceedings of the 2002 International Joint Conference on, 2002.

[21] F. Kaytez, M. C. Taplamacioglu, E. Cam, and F. Hardalac, "Forecasting electricity consumption: a comparison of regression analysis, neural networks and least squares support vector machines," International Journal of Electrical Power and Energy Systems, vol. 67, 431-438, 2015.

[22] G. Zanghirati, and L. Zanni, "A parallel solver for large quadratic programs in training support vector machines," Parallel computing, vol. 29(4), 535-551, 2003.

[23] R. Collobert, S. Bengio, and Y. Bengio, "A parallel mixture of SVMs for very large scale problems," Neural computation, vol. 14(5), 1105-1114, 2002.

[24] J. x. Dong, A. Krzyżak, and C. Y. Suen, "A fast parallel optimization for training support vector machine Machine Learning and Data Mining in Pattern Recognition," Springer, 96-105, 2003.

[25] L. Zanni, T. Serafini, and G. Zanghirati, "Parallel software for training large scale support vector machines on multiprocessor systems," The Journal of Machine Learning Research, vol. 7, 1467-1492, 2006.

[26] C. L. Blake and C.J. Merz, UCI repository of machine learning databases. from http://www.ics.uci.edu/~mlearn/MLRepository.html, 1998, [accessed June 2017].

A Study of Extracting Demands of Social Media Fans

Chih-Chuan Chen
Interdisciplinary Program of Green and Information Technology
National Taitung University
Taitung, Taiwan, R.O.C.
e-mail: ccchen@nttu.edu.tw

Chien-Wei He
Institute of Information Management
National Cheng Kung University
Tainan City, Taiwan, R.O.C.
e-mail: simulatedmsn@gmail.com

Hui-Chi Chuang
Institute of Information Management
National Cheng Kung University
Tainan City, Taiwan, R.O.C.
e-mail: huichi613@gmail.com

Sheng-Tun Li
Institute of Information Management, Department of Industrial and Information Management
National Cheng Kung University
Tainan City, Taiwan, R.O.C.
e-mail: stli@mail.ncku.edu.tw

***Abstract*—With the boom of the Internet era, people spend more and more time on social media, such as Facebook, Twitter, and Tumblr. How to get people's attention is becoming a critical issue for companies and celebrities, since it is an era of distractions. In the past, if a company wanted to become popular, it simply spent money on traditional media, like newspapers or TV commercials. Now, one has to know audiences' needs and then utilize the new social media platforms to reach those specific audiences. How to know the demand of customers (audiences) is an unavoidable challenge? To answer that question, most commonly used methods are conducting market surveys, including questionnaires and focus groups. However, it is not only time wasting but also effort consuming. In this paper, we combine text mining techniques and Kansei engineering to analyze audiences' demand. Firstly, we collect data from Facebook Fan Pages, including numerical data (number of likes, shares, comments) and text data (postcontent). Secondly, we extract the topics by using Latent Dirichlet Allocation (LDA). Thirdly, experts will give eight pairs of Kansei words that are most relevant to the articles. Finally, we produce a semantic differential questionnaire to find the relationship between topics and Kansei words. The relationship can give helpful insights into the demands of the audience. Moreover, a supervised LDA is incorporated in this approach to predict the popularity of posts.**

Keywords—Kansei engineering; topic model; text mining; demand analysis

I. INTRODUCTION

How can I become famous? This is a question that every author asks himself or herself. Traditionally, a writer signs a contract with a publishing house, and then the publishing house harnesses their own channels to promote the writer's books. Nowadays, with the boom of the Web and social media, writers must cultivate online channels, as well. According to a recent survey by the Market Intelligence and Consulting Institute (MIT) in Taiwan [1], the top five most used social media platforms, in order, are Facebook (95.8%), Google+ (24.7%), Pixnet (20.7%), Xuite (12.7%), Plurk (8%). The top three discussion groups are Mobile01 (51.4%), NTU PTT (51.2%), Yahoo Knowledge+ (46.2%). Accordingly, there are both opportunities and challenges for writers. If writers can devote themselves to managing a social-media platform, they will gain popularity, which may boost their next publication sales. Conversely, the next book sales may not improve if the writers do not pay attention to their online platform.

In this respect, some proactive writers take advantage of social media, and post some parts of their publications to the Web, then track the audiences' reactions. If the audience enjoys the post's content, they might write more about it, and vice versa. Some famous examples of such an approach include Giddens Ko, Hiyawu and Riff Raff Tsai. Once the online popularity has accumulated, they will publish a paper book via the offline channel.

Among online publications, one branch has been rising, which is called "healing essay". In the contemporary era, people feel more pressure than before; thus, "healing" became a popular topic. On Google Trends, a search for the keyword 'healing' shows that the search volume has increased year after year since 2011. This trend has resulted in many products, such as the "healing picture book", "healing music" and "healing app". The healing essay also fits within this healing category. Moreover, the healing essay can make people feel better or inspired when they are struggling with depression and pressure.

Although we are well aware of the importance of social media, its operation is still difficult for writers and publishing houses. The main challenge is that people's demands are not particularly clear. Data collected by social media are unstructured and text-based, which creates difficulty when analyzing people's demands. In order to better analyze the demand, some people will use Kansei engineering, but doing so is time-consuming. As such, in this study, we use Latent Dirichlet Allocation (LDA), a probability language model, to reduce the time needed to obtain factors for why some essays are so attractive [2].

In this paper, we endeavor to build a framework to characterize the demand of the audience and the popularity of articles. We introduce Kansei Engineering and LDA to extract the Kansei words and topics. After experts turn the identified Kansei words into topic names, we conduct semantic differential questionnaires to highlight the relationships between topics and Kansei words.

II. Literature Review

A. Text Mining

In the previous data mining study, researchers focused on numerical data that came from the relational database. Nowadays, we find that around 85~90% of data are stored in unstructured format [3], such as emails, customer's comments, and PDF files. In addition, this data usually contains a large amount of important information; yet understanding it by computer is challenging. As a result, text mining has become increasingly common in recent years. Text mining is also known as knowledge discovery in textual databases, and can be applied to many areas.

For instance, Jin, Ji, Liu, and Johnson Lim [3] translated online customer opinions into engineering characteristics, which is an important step in Quality Function Deployment (QFD). In the traditional QFD method, to digest customer reviews into useful information is a time-consuming and labor-intensive process. In Jin's study, 770 printer reviews were collected from Amazon and Epson's website, and it took more than two weeks to translate the reviews.

The second example is Popescu's research [4], in which epochs of human history were automatically defined. Conventionally, the definition of an epoch relies on historians' knowledge and observations of extended time periods. However, it is difficult to define such epochs objectively and no standard measurement to support their opinions exists. Therefore, the research team decided to use Google n-gram to find evidence of epochs changing. Google n-gram is a part of the Google Books project, and counts any word or short sentence yearly in sources printed from the 6th century to the 21st century, where n represents the length of segmentation. For example, 1-gram means to separate each word in the sentence; 2-grams mean two words will become a group (e.g., "what do", "do you", "you need"). The researchers employed many statistic measurements to identify significant changes in word frequencies.

B. Kansei Engineering

Kansei Engineering (KE) is a method to convert consumers' feelings and images for products into design elements [5]. Kansei is an ergonomics and consumer-oriented approach for producing new products [6] and is defined as "translating the customers' Kansei into the product design domain" [5]. In other words, Kansei is applied to translate the feelings and images of customers regarding what they want, need, and demand into the product design field, including product mechanical function [6]. KE can be applied to many areas, such as door design [7], kitchen design [8], housing design [9], [10]

However, to the best of our knowledge, there are no studies that have investigated the transiting audiences' Kansei to article design. In recent years, social media growth has been phenomenal, with more and more people sharing their status and feelings on the Web. When they share their bad situations, they are actually searching for someone to give a positive reply. Sometimes, this reply will have healing effects to those people in need. Such responses are called 'healing essays' in this paper.

C. Topic Model

Topic model, which is widely used in machine learning and in Natural Language Processing (NLP) areas, is a generative model in statistical theory. The purposes of the topic model are to discover the latent semantics (latent topics) within a corpus, and to build a generative model through those latent topics. Topic model applies various probability distributions to constructing the generative model, which could deal with the semantic problem better, like synonym and polysemy. The two most common topic model are Probabilistic latent semantic analysis (PLSA) and LDA [2].

PLSA extends the concept of latent semantic analysis (LSA) using statistical view [11]. Instead of SVD, PLSA employs aspect model as its main structure. Aspect model is a latent variable model which represents the latent semantic relation within observed data by probability function. Then maximum likelihood estimation is used for inferring the parameters of PLSA model.

Latent Dirichlet allocation is a probabilistic generative model of a corpus, which can solve the problems that PLSA suffers from. In addition, PLSA is a special case of LDA [2]. In LDA, each document is considered as a mixture model that is constructed by random latent topic, and each latent topic is characterized by a distribution over words. LDA applies a three layers' representation to a corpus, and employs different probabilistic distributions between layers. Recently, some research has shown that LDA performs well in natural language model [12], [13] and machine learning areas [14].

Most topic model are unsupervised, just like the LDA. However, in a realistic world, some corpus is labeled, which means that each document belongs to one category. Mcauliffe and Blei proposed an improved version of LDA in 2008 [15]. This method can let us deal with labeled data. We use response to denote the labeled value, and the value can be categories, ordered class label, and real values.

The generative process of each document is similar to LDA, but it adds a response variable. It also uses E-M algorithm to maximize the likelihood function. The Supervised Latent Dirichlet Allocation (SLDA) method has better performance than traditional LDA method, since the response will help the process of LDA.

III. Research Method

A. Data Collection

Facebook was launched in 2004 by Mark Zuckerberg and was opened in Taiwan in 2006. After one decade, Facebook has become the most popular social network in Taiwan. People use Facebook to share opinions, check in, update their recent status, and most *importantly, read news feed.*

Facebook also has Pages for companies and celebrities. Businesses have found it to be a good channel to broadcast their ideas and promote their products. In recent years, some bloggers and popular writers have used Pages as a platform to communicate with their fans.

B. Data Preprocessing

In this paper, the collected corpus was Mandarin Chinese (hereafter referred to as simply Chinese). How to correctly segment sentences into words is an important task. In English, white space can be used as an indicator to cut sentences into words; however, white space do not exist in Chinese sentences. Thanks to efforts of previous researchers, there are many tools that can deal with this problem, such as CKIP (provided by Academia Sinica), Stanford Parser (provided by Stanford NLP group), and Jieba (provided by Sun Junyi).

The preprocessing process can be divided into four steps. The first and second steps involve building the Netizen-words list and Stop-words list, respectively. Then, the third step is segmentation, which is followed by the final step of P-O-S (part of speech) tagging. A more detailed explanation is given below.

Netizen-words list: Many Chinese segmentation tools are based on their training corpus (term dictionary) to obtain better results. As time goes by, more and more special terms are used by netizens. Such terms usually have a particular meaning, such as "BJ4" , which means 'no need to explain'. If those terms can be collected as a list and provided to a segmentation tool, the accuracy of the results can be greatly enhanced. In other words, we can obtain the right terms from sentences.

Stop-words list Commonly-used words, punctuation and meaningless words (such as "of") should be removed during the segmentation step. If those words do not get filtered, the segmentation results will contain many useless terms, which will unnecessarily increase the computation loading. Thus, a stop-words list must be built beforehand.

Segmentation: Among the many segmentation tools, we chose Jieba in this paper, the main reason for which is because it is an open source tool that allows code modification if needed. This tool can load users own dictionaries, stop-words list, etc. Although Jieba can interpret unknown words by using Hidden Markov Model (HMM), offer dictionary (netizen-words list and stop-words list) can enhance the performance.

P-O-S tagging: P-O-S tagging is an abbreviation for part-of-speech tagging. In the following Kansei engineering step, we need to distinguish adjectives from sentences.

C. Topic Extraction

In order to extract the topics of every article, we use the LDA algorithm. The LDA input can be divided into four levels, as illustrated in Figure 1. The Documents level is the set of every separate document. We segmented the documents into words to create the Words level. The Dictionary level is the set of all words in each document, for which each unique word was given a unique ID. The final level is creating the corpus, for which the word frequency of each document was counted.

After processing the documents, we needed to set the initial parameter of the LDA algorithm. Following Steyvers and Griffiths, we set α=50/k & β=0.01 [16].

The next step of the LDA involved using the expectation-maximization (EM) algorithm to optimize the parameters. The LDA outputs are two matrices, where one is a document-topic matrix and the other is a topic-word matrix. The values of the document-topic matrix denote the probability distribution between documents and latent topics. The values of the topic-word matrix denote the probability distribution between latent topics and words.

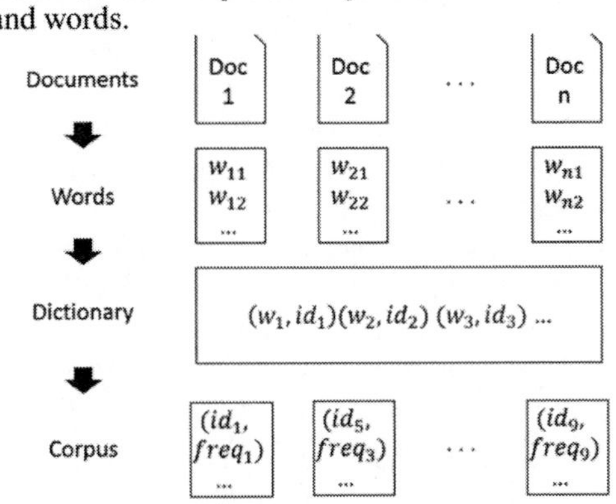

Figure 1. Input of LDA

Experts still need to define the topics' names. After reading a couple words from each topic, experts give a name that can represent the general concept of each topic.

D. Semantic Differential

Semantic differential is a general method for measuring people's attitudes or feelings. This method was proposed by C. E Osgoods and G. J. Suci in 1957 [17], and often uses a questionnaire to characterize respondents' emotions through a series of polarization scales. Semantic differential comprises three parts, namely concept, scale and subject. Concepts are for evaluating targets. In this paper, the concepts are topics extracted in the previous step. The scale is composed of two different adjectives, such as important and unimportant. The final part is subjects, which refers to sample size.

We use semantic differential to analyze whether the topics extracted by LDA are important to the audience or not.

IV. Experiment and Analysis

In this section, we record the results of each step during the experiment and conduct an analysis of the results

A. Experiment

Among the many popular writers, we chose Little Lifer as our study target. Little Lifer is a writer in Taiwan, and his posts are written in Chinese. Therefore, we implemented all the experiments by using Chinese articles. There are three reasons we chose Little Lifer. First, he rose to fame from the Web, therefore, the vast majority of his fans comes from the Web. Second, Little Lifer's Facebook Page has been growing since January 2015, and as of April, 2016, has been liked by 68,000 people. And third, a netizen writer can provide more measurable data from the Web, such as the number of likes and the number of fans.

Among the data collected from Little Lifer, each post can be categorized into three types: Status, Photo and Link. Since this paper focuses on the articles part, which often comprises long articles to help with Netizen's problems, we filtered all other posts. We deleted each data row except the post message containing "Reply".

Textual data were collected within Little Lifer's replies on PTT (the biggest forum in Taiwan). There are a total of 88 articles, 67 of which are also posted on Facebook. At first, we saved each article in a separate file. As mentioned above, Jieba was used to segment the words after loading the Netizen-words list and Stop-words list. The Netizen-words list contained 255 terms frequently used by netizens and Little Lifer. On the other hand, the Stop-words list consisted of 22 punctuation marks and meaningless words. During the segmentation process, we simultaneously performed P-O-S tagging.

TABLE I. ARTICLES SUMMARY OF TERMS COUNT

# Articles		All terms	Adj.	Noun
88 (PTT)	total	47214	1940	9560
	Average	537	22	109
67 (Facebook)	total	36061	1479	7249
	Average	538	22	108

After the process, 44,214 and 36,061 terms were obtained from PTT and Facebook, respectively. The term count summary is shown in TABLE In examining Little Lifer ' s articles more closely on Facebook, we found that 27% of his articles are composed by 301~400 terms, and 24% by 401~500 terms. In other words, about half of his articles contained less than 500 terms, which indicates that Little Lifer tends to write short articles to help his readers.

In this section, we use LDA to automatically generate article topics. Initially, we put each term into the corpus to generate topics, for which the number of topics was set at 4. In doing so, a list of topics was obtained. We generated topics by using all terms, adjectives, nouns, and a mix of nouns, verbs, and adjectives.

After examining the topic composition presented above, we decided to use the adjective topics as our corpus input. There are two primary reasons for choosing adjectives as our input are as follows. Firstly, adjectives are more representative to people's Kansei attributes; if we read an adjective, we can interpret the meaning immediately. Secondly, adjectives are easier for experts to label; knowing the general concept behind those grouped adjectives is more straightforward.

Then, we changed the number of topics from 4 to 8, which means that totally 5 topics were produced. We sent those results to Little Lifer, who played the role of expert in our study. He suggested that we should try to set 4 as our number of topics, since he thought it would be easier to label each composition. After labeling, we obtained our topic model for Little Lifer's articles (Figure 2). In the next section, we utilize the Kansei engineering process to gain more insight into our topic model.

Figure 2. Topic Model of articles

In order to better understand readers' Kansei feeling toward the different topics listed in the prior section, a Kansei semantic differential questionnaire was conducted. The questionnaire consisted of two parts.

The first part was the design object. In normal Kansei engineering, this can be furniture, residences, cars, etc. In this study, we treated articles as design objects. Then, we took each article's topic composition as the object elements. Because we set the number of topics at four, we selected four articles in each topic cluster.

The second part is Kansei words. After reviewing the topic composition, the expert gave us eight pairs of Kansei words, as displayed in TABLE II . Each pair of Kansei words is made up of two different words.

TABLE II. KANSEI WORD PAIRS

Pairs		Pairs	
Rational	Sensible	Be healed	Be reprimanded
Sincere	Pretentious	Touching	Funny
Humor	Rigid	Irrelevant	Straightforward
Constructive	Colloquial	Helpful	Unhelpful

This semantic differential questionnaire was posted on Little Lifer' Facebook Pages. Finally, we obtained 549 copies of the questionnaire, the validity criteria of which is described below.

B. Analysis

Initially, we needed to remove some copies of the questionnaire due to responding time constraints. There were two criteria for removing questionnaires, as explained in the following. Firstly, our questionnaire respondent needed to read four articles sequentially. We assumed that each article required about two minutes; that is to say, each questionnaire required at least eight minutes to be finished. We used quartiles according to filling time to divide the questionnaire answers into four parts. Then, we removed the questionnaires for which filling time was less than Q1 (25% was removed). For the second criterion, we removed the questionnaires for which filling time was relatively longer than the normal situation (over one hour). After reviewing the filling time, we decided to delete the questionnaires for which the filling time was longer than one hour. After these two steps, 380 valid questionnaires remained, which constituted a validity rate of about 69%.

To determine whether the mean between the different topics is the same or not, we conducted an analysis of variance (ANOVA). We set eight hypotheses as below:

$$H_{0,i}: \mu_{1,i} = \mu_{2,i} = \mu_{3,i} = \mu_{4,i}$$

where μ denotes the mean of each topic, for which the range of each topic was between 1 to 4. The variable, i, denotes each question for different Kansei words, where the range of i is from 1 to 8. The value of significant of each hypotheses are below 0.05.

As displayed in Figure 3, we can find that the four topics have different Kansei feeling towards the audience. For example, topic 2 (sincerely description) is more touching than topic 1 (tender loving care). Namely, if the writer wants to give the reader a touching feeling, he or she can choose sincerely description as the main topic.

In order to predict whether the Facebook post would be popular or not, we used SLDA to predict the like rate. At first, we used the interquartile range to discretize the Y value (like rate) into four labels, as in TABLE III. Then, we used different numbers of topics and parts of speech in the corpus as the control variables, respectively. The results were validated by 10-fold cross validation, a common validation method adopted in the data mining area. The experiment setting is exemplified with SLDA Experiment Setting - 1 in TABLE IV.

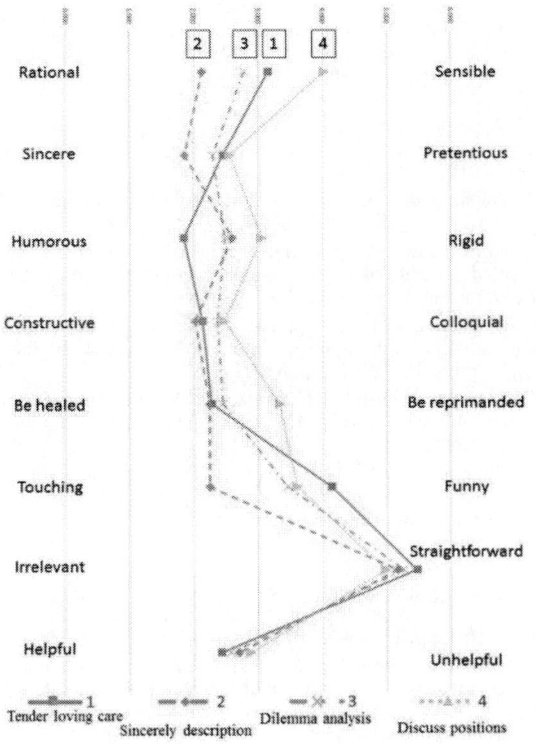

Figure 3. Topic-Kansei Relationship

TABLE III. LABELS OF Y VALUES

Interquartile range	Percentage	Labels
Q1	0%~25%	Very low
Q2	26%~50%	Low
Q3	51%~75%	High
Q4	76~100%	Very High

TABLE IV. SLDA EXPERIMENT SETTING - 1

Experiment name	adj_4type	all_4type
Number of topics	3 ~ 55	3 ~ 55
Part of speech	Adjective	Use all terms
Validation method	10-fold cross validation	10-fold cross validation

The results are presented in Figure 4. As can be seen, when the number of topics was relatively low, using adjectives can yield better performance. Moreover, as the number of topics increased when all terms were used, the value of R-square also increased. Accordingly, the more words we used, the greater the number of topics needed when using the SLDA model.

The second experiment compared SLDA, support vector regression (SVR), and linear regression, the experiment settings of which are shown in TABLE V.

As shown in Figure 5, SLDA outperforms SVR and linear regression. As such, we conducted a hypothesis test between SLDA and SVR, where μ represents the mean value of R-square. Analysis results showed that the p-value was smaller than 0.05 in TABLE VI and so H_0 was rejected. In other words, SLDA had better performance than SVR.

$$H_0:\ \mu_{slda} \leq \mu_{svr}$$
$$H_1:\ \mu_{slda} > \mu_{svr}$$

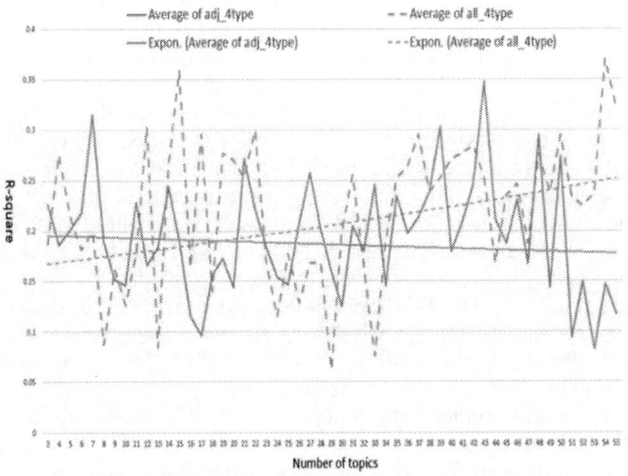

Figure 4. Results of SLDA experiment setting - 1

TABLE V. SLDA EXPERIMENT SETTING - 2

Experiment name	SLDA	SVR	LR
Predicting method	Supervised LDA	Support vector regression	Linear Regression
Number of topics	3 ~ 55	3 ~ 55	3 ~ 55
Part of speech	Adjective	Adjective	Adjective
Validation method	10-fold cross validation	10-fold cross validation	10-fold cross validation

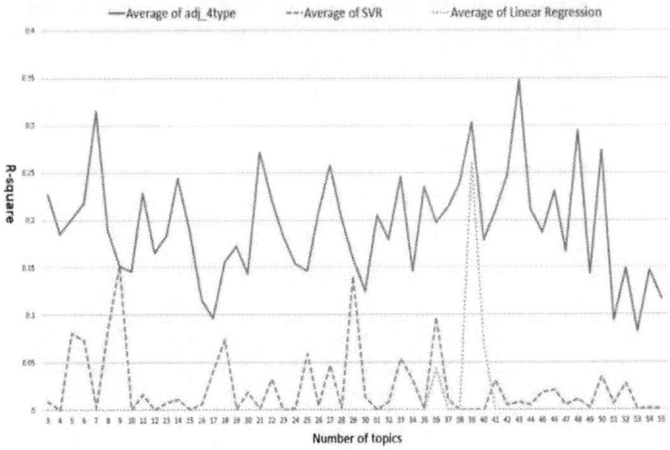

Figure 5. Comparison between SLDA, SVR, and Linear Regression

TABLE VI. ANOVA TABLE OF SLDA AND SVR

Source of Variation	SS	df	MS	F	P-value
Between Groups	0.771	1	0.771	3.932	**8.250E-35**
Within Groups	0.232	104	0.002		
Total	1.003	105			

V. Conclusion and Future Work

A. Conclusion

Topic modeling is a widely applied technique in many areas for finding the latent topics of documents. Kansei engineering is a method aiming at the development or improvement of products and services by translating the customer's psychological feelings and needs into the domain of product design. In this study, we combined LDA and Kansei engineering to analyze the need of audience of social media fan page. Firstly, we collected numerical data and textual data from both Facebook and PTT. Secondly, LDA is used to generate topics with different contents. The contents were divided into four groups, including only nouns, only adjectives, and sets of nouns, verb and adjectives, and all terms. We found that using only adjectives generated the best topic models. After discussing the results with the expert, we included four topics in our corpus. The four topics were tender loving care, sincere description, dilemma analysis and discuss positions. Thirdly, we chose articles within different topics and conducted semantic differential questionnaires. In this step, a topic-Kansei relationship model was built, so we could know reader's Kansei feeling given any new articles. Finally, an SLDA model was built to predict whether a post would be popular or not. We also found that using only adjectives to generate topics is superior to using all terms when the number of topics is relatively low.

B. Future Work

The main purpose of this paper was to introduce a method that helps writers become more popular. However, some issues remain to be solved in the future.

1. The corpus of this study contained only 67 articles, which is relatively small compared to most text mining research. If a larger corpus is provided, better performance on topic modeling would be obtained.
2. The proposed model in this study was tested with only one writer. This model should be applied to other writers in the future to determine its validity.
3. The topic model was generated by one writer. In the future, a holistic topic model could be built using a group of different writers.

Acknowledgment

This study was supported in part by the Ministry of Science and Technology, ROC, under contract MOST 105-2410-H-143-020. The authors also thank Mr. Chien-Wei He for his help on the experimentation.

References

[1] MIC., "96.2%台灣網友近期曾使用社交網站," Market Intelligence & Consulting Institute. Retrieved from http://mic.iii.org.tw/intelligence/pressroom/pop_pressfull.asp?sno=364, 2014.

[2] D. M. Blei, A. Y. Ng, and M. I. Jordan, "Latent dirichlet allocation. the Journal of machine Learning research," vol. 3, pp. 993-1022, 2003.

[3] W. McKnight, "Text Data Mining in Business Intelligence," Information Management Magazine. Retrieved from http://www.information-management.com/issues/20050101/1016487-1.html, 2005.

[4] O. Popescu, and C. Strapparava, "Time corpora: Epochs, opinions and changes," Knowledge-Based Systems, vol. 69, pp. 3-13, 2014.

[5] M. Nagamachi, "Introduction of Kansei engineering," Japan Standard Association, Tokyo, 1996.

[6] M. Nagamachi, "Kansei engineering as a powerful consumer-oriented technology for product development," Applied ergonomics, vol. 33(3), pp. 289-294, 2002.

[7] Y. Matsubara, and M. Nagamachi, "Hybrid Kansei engineering system and design support," International Journal of Industrial Ergonomics, vol. 19(2), pp. 81-92, 1997a.

[8] Y. Matsubara, and M. Nagamachi, "Kansei analysis support system and virtual kes," Kansei Engineering I, Kaibundo, pp. 53-62, 1997b.

[9] C. Llinares, and A. Page, "Application of product differential semantics to quantify purchaser perceptions in housing assessment," Building and environment, vol. 42(7), pp. 2488-2497, 2007.

[10] C. Llinares, and A. F. Page, "Kano's model in Kansei Engineering to evaluate subjective real estate consumer preferences," International Journal of Industrial Ergonomics, vol. 41(3), pp. 233-246, 2011.

[11] T. Hofmann, "Probabilistic latent semantic indexing," Paper presented at the Proceedings of the 22nd annual international ACM SIGIR conference on Research and development in information retrieval, 1999.

[12] D. Mrva, and P. C. Woodland, "Unsupervised language model adaptation for Mandarin broadcast conversation transcription," Paper presented at the INTERSPEECH, 2006.

[13] Y. C. Tam, and T. Schultz, "Dynamic language model adaptation using variational Bayes inference," Paper presented at the INTERSPEECH, 2005.

[14] D. M. Blei, and J. D. Lafferty, "Dynamic topic models," Paper presented at the Proceedings of the 23rd international conference on Machine learning, 2006.

[15] J. D. Mcauliffe, and D. M. Blei, "Supervised topic models," Paper presented at the Advances in neural information processing systems, 2008.

[16] M. Steyvers, and T. Griffiths, "Probabilistic topic models," Handbook of latent semantic analysis, vol. 427(7), pp. 424-440, 2007.

[17] C. E. Osgood, G. J. Suci, ,and P. H. Tannenbaum, "The Measurement of Meaning," Urbana, IL: University of Illinois Press, 1957.

How Happiness Affects Travel Decision Making

Sz-Meng Yang
Institute of the Law of the Sea
National Taiwan Ocean University
Keelung, Taiwan, R.O.C.
e-mail: abc0931881057@hotmail.com

Pei-Chih Chen
Department of Product Design
Tainan University of Technology
Tainan City, Taiwan, R.O.C.
e-mail: t00195@mail.tut.edu.tw

Ruei-Ying Ching
Department of Technology Management
Chung Hua University
Hsinchu, Taiwan, R.O.C.
e-mail: jangel580707@yahoo.com.tw

***Abstract*— Consumer's definition of happiness affects their product choices; therefore, firms try to portray a happy image of their products. The sense of happiness varies depending on our temporal focus. Young people are more focused on the future and their feelings of happiness lead to excitement, and, therefore, they tend to choose exciting products. On the other hand, older people are more focused on the present, therefore, incline to choose a calm product. Nowadays, in the tourism industry, more and more customers pay attention to the psychological level of satisfaction. This study explores the definition of happiness and temporal focus in terms of journey which influence consumers' choice of tourism products. We also observe whether the change of definition of happiness affects the choice of journey between the old and young people. Two experiments were conducted on two groups of students, one consisting of the graduate students and the other consisting of the members of the senior citizens learning camp, from a university of technology in southern Taiwan. The results could give some suggestions to tourism industry to provide more enjoyable products to customers.**

Keywords- happiness; calm; excitement; temporal focus.

I. INTRODUCTION

Nowadays, enterprises begin to take into account consumers' definition of happiness when developing marketing strategies. For example, HOLA [1] uses the advertising slogan "To create a new relationship we love, you and I are happy to get married!" Convenience store, 7-Eleven, uses the slogan "The familiar warmth, a brand new taste. The warmth in the hands is the real happiness in the heart." to promote "Kanto-Daki", a famous dish originally from Kanto area in Japan. CHIMEI Group [2] uses "Giving her all she wants to see is happiness. Giving her all the wishes is a luxurious happiness" as slogan to promote their LCD TV screen.

In some situations, the type of happiness is determined by the temporal focus. When consumers focus on the future, they incline to choose an exciting option. On the other hand, when consumers focus on the present, they prefer to choose a calm option. Therefore, this study explores how the definition of happiness and temporal focus affect tourists' choice of itinerary. The results of the experiment could help the tourism industry design customized itineraries based on the need of customers. In addition, people can choose their favorite itineraries depending on their definition of happiness.

In this research, we observed that young people are more focused on the future than their elder counterparts, who are more focused on the present moment. Moreover, the definition of happiness of the young generations is more related to excitement, while that of the elder ones is more related to calmness. We also observed how the temporal focus affects people's definition of happiness and choice of tourism products, as well as the impact of the change of the temporal focus.

In order to verify the hypothesis, this study conducted two experiments using two groups of research objects, one consisting of the graduate students and the other consisting of the members of the senior citizens learning camp from a university of technology in southern Taiwan. In both experiments, the temporal focus of elderly and graduate students was controlled to verify whether temporal focus would affect the definition of happiness and the choice between excitement and calmness. In the first experiment, graduate students were influenced by focusing on the present. In the second experiment, elderly students were influenced by focusing on the future. In both experiments, we explore how people define happiness, as well as observe their choice of calm or exciting journeys. In the experiments, the types of journeys were unknown to the objects. The journeys were designed during the same periods of time while the price was not considered.

The rest of the paper is structured as follows. In Section II, we present literature review. In Section III, we describe research method. The experiment and discussion are shown in Section IV. Finally, we present the conclusion and future work in Section V.

II. LITERATURE REVIEW

Happiness is abstract and concrete at the same time. It has a nature of singularity as well as diversity. It is a feeling and it is also a scenario. Despite the fact that people are constantly pursuing happiness, they do not know happiness is quietly controlling our decision. What is happiness? Happiness is a dream of almost every one. However, the definition of happiness varies from person to person. There are many kinds of definitions of happiness, such as being healthy, being accompanied by family or friends, and having a sumptuous dinner. It does not require exquisiteness to enhance happiness. Happiness could be simple, and be happy just because of some ordinary things. Therefore, there is no standard for the real definition of happiness.

Merriam [3] defined happiness as "a state of health and happiness and satisfaction; a pleasant or satisfying experience". So, happiness can be a state of feelings, and it also can be an experience. Some scholars believe that happiness is a singularity that means for everyone happiness is the same [4], [5]. On the contrary, some scholars believe that happiness is subjective and various. According to their study, happiness is different for each person [6]. In some research, happiness is classified into two categories of positive emotions. The first one includes excitement, joy, and passion. This type of emotional response is defined as the positive effect of "high arousal". The second one includes calm, serene, quiet, and ordinary. This kind of mood is defined as "low arousal" [7], [8], [9].

However, age can be a proxy mechanism for the "temporal focus" of the individual's underlying psychological factors. In other words, when a person is young, the temporal focus will fall on the more excited sense of happiness. So, people incline to seek novel and helpful information for the future. Naturally the attention of young people will focus on the future. On the contrary, when a person is older, his/her temporal focus will fall on more calm sense of happiness, because to the elders it is the most important to enjoy the present moment. Therefore, personal happiness experience may come from the temporal focus, rather than age itself. Even though the age may be a useful signal of personal temporal focusing, the personal emphasis on the future or the present is to determine its happiness linked to excitement or calm.

A person's mood may affect a person's perception of things, as well as their choice of type. For example, when a person holds positive emotions, he/she would mostly take heuristic approaches [10]. Heuristic approaches, also called tactical approaches, usually refer to finding the solutions based on limited knowledge or incomplete information, in a short period of time. For example, when making a decision on where to go the ski trip between South Korea or Japan, one finds that the yen depreciated significantly and hence, chooses to travel to Japan. This reasonable process is a typical heuristic approach.

When in a good mood, one would tend to be optimistic about the future, and will not pay attention to immediate concerns, and naturally, will think on the bright side [11]. Regardless of the way a choice is made, the positive emotions are directly affecting the choice. In addition, happiness has singularity and diversity at the same time, that is, some may have the same definition of happiness while some may have different definitions of happiness. Therefore, one would ask whether a person's happiness plays a role in selecting a specific option? If so, how does it affect the choice? For example, when someone defines happiness as calm, he would incline to choose a calm product, such as static journey.

According to previous studies, happiness can be classified into two categories, namely, excitement and calm which not only affect the consumer choice of products, but also affect the consumer evaluation of the products. The tourism industry should classify the customers based on the two types of definition of happiness, and furthermore design favorable tourism products for both types of customers.

To see if guiding the calm consumer to choose more a calmer journey with the proper advertisements is reasonable, we propose the first hypothesis.

H_1: The definition of happiness will affect the choice, (a) when happiness is close to excitement, one is more likely to choose an exciting option than a calm option; (b) when the happiness is close to calm, one is more likely to choose a more calming, rather than exciting, option .

In addition to the excitement and calm moods, it is also shown that "age is a potential psychological factor - temporal focus." For example, in the choice of diet, young people will choose delicious food and elder people will choose healthy and light food. In the choice of brands, elder people tend to choose familiar and conservative options while young people will tend to choose a new, creative, unknown brand. Therefore, we assume that temporal focus will influence the choice because of the situational factors, and then form the second hypothesis of this study. Assume that when the focus is on the future, happiness is defined as the feeling of excitement, and consumers will tend to choose the exciting option. Suppose that when the focus is on the present, happiness is defined as calm feeling, and consumers will be more likely to choose a calm option.

H_2: Temporal focus affects selection, (a) when the temporal focus is set in the future, the likelihood of choosing an exciting product is greater than the calm ones; (b) when the temporal focus is set in the present, the probability of choosing a calm product is greater than the exciting ones.

Figure 1 displays the conceptual model of the effects of temporal focus on happiness and choice constructed by H_1 and H_2.

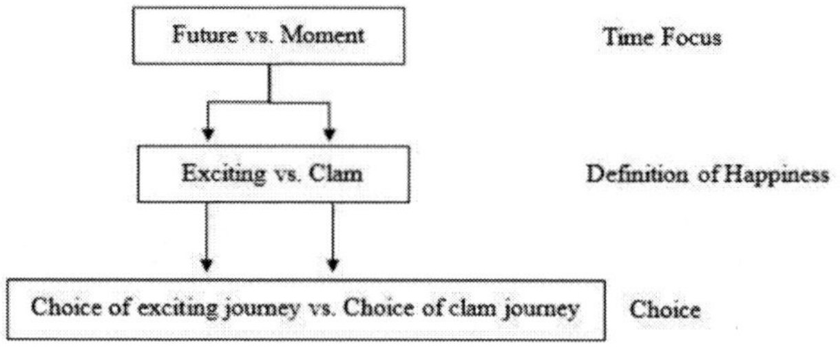

Figure 1. The framework of temporal focus to Happiness and Choice [12]

III. RESEARCH METHODOLOGY

In this study, young people are more focused on the future than elder people. The tendency, that the elderly define happiness as calm, is greater than that of the young people. In the experiment, we also observed that whether the change of temporal focus will affect the definition of happiness and the choice between exciting or calm. In this study, the journey is designed as 15 days package tour to

Europe (calm journey) and 15 days of self-service tour to Europe (exciting journey).

A. *Experiment 1: Graduate students and the choice between exciting or calm journey*

The experiment is divided into two parts, experiment 1-1 and experiment 1-2. The subjects are graduate students of a southern University of Technology. Experiment 1-1 used "Happy McDonald's" breakfast as subject. A fast-food breakfast can make people feel excited when they finish their meal. The researchers began to introduce the design of the two journeys for them to select. After a few days, we conducted experiment 1-2. We invited the same subjects to participate in "Coffee of the day". This was an activity about providing them free breakfast at Starbucks. In the leisurely morning, they stayed at a quiet coffee shop and enjoyed coffee or tea to relax.

After finishing the meal, the researcher introduced the two pre-designed journey and questionnaires. Participants were asked to choose the trip they want to attend. Experiment 1 was finished. The purpose of this experiment was to know whether the journey of the chosen student is different from the one chosen for "Happy McDonald's" after the graduate students had been guided into a calm situation. That is, whether the graduate students change the definition of happiness or not by changing the temporal focus.

B. *Experiment 2: Elderly students and the choice between exciting or calm journey*

The experiment is divided into two parts, experiment 2-1 and experiment 2-2. The subjects are elderly people in a southern University of Technology. In experiment 2-1, they do a spiritual and meditation course for 30 minutes. Meditation had been proven to change one's temporal focus and guide them more easily towards a calm happiness [13], [14]. When the course was completed, the researcher introduced the two pre-designed journeys and the questionnaires. Participants were asked to choose the journey they want to participate in. In experiment 2-2, the elderly participants enjoyed the final carnival dinner. The interaction between the participants during the dinner helped to achieve the effect of excitement. After that, the researcher introduced these two pre-designed journeys and the questionnaires. The participants were asked to choose the journey they want to join.

IV. EXPERIMENTS AND DISCUSSION

The subjects of this experiment were graduate and elderly students in the southern university of technology. There are 17 graduate students and they are between 22 and 24 years old. There are 30 elderly students and they are between 50 and 99 years old.

A. *Experiment 1: Graduate students are about the Choice of Excitement and Calm journey*

In experiment 1-1, subjects are graduate students. Before the experiment, they are young and their temporal focus is on future, so they defined happiness as excitement. After the "Happy McDonald's" experiment, the definition of happiness was guided to excitement, and the condition was achieved. Six questionnaires were conducted on the same day and all of them were valid. From the questionnaire, we asked "Is there any excitement in the activities of the "Happy McDonald's"? Six graduate students believed that the activities will lead them to excitement. Thus, the results of this study show that there were two possibilities. One was changing the definition of happiness by the McDonald's happy atmosphere for graduate students. Another was that graduate students are more interested in an exciting journey when the temporal focus is on the future. The results are shown in Table I.

TABLE I. HAPPY MCDONALD'S EXPERIMENT STATISTIC TABLE

Happiness \ Journey	calm	excitement	Total
calm	0	0	0
excitement	1	5	6
Total	1	5	6

Next, in experiment 1-2, subjects are graduate students, and they are young and temporal focus is on the future, so they defined happiness as excited. After the "Coffee of the Day" experiment, the definition of happiness was successfully guided to calm. There were 12 questionnaires be conducted on the same day and 10 of them were valid, 2 were invalid. From the questionnaire, we asked "Is there any calm in the activities of the "Coffee of the Day"? From Table II, there are eight graduate students choose exciting journey. Thus, the results of this study showed that there are two possibilities. One is that the "Coffee of the Day" calm atmosphere changed the definition of happiness for graduate students. The other one is that, no matter how happiness is defined, the temporal focus on the future is more significant.

TABLE II. COFFEE OF THE DAY EXPERIMENT STATISTIC TABLE

Happiness \ Journey	calm	excitement	Total
calm	0	2	2
excitement	0	8	8
Total	0	10	10

B. Experiment 2: Elderly students and the choice between exciting or calm journey

The subjects are elderly students in the University of Technology of South Taiwan in experiment 2-1. They are older and focused on the moment and define happiness as a calm feeling. In the beginning, the elderly students were invited to participate in an activity about "mental and physical peace and meditation" and guided students to define happiness as a sense of calmness. From the 22 questionnaires distributed, 14 of them were valid and 8 were invalid. The questionnaire asked "Is there any calm in meditation?". Among these 14 valid questionnaires, there were 13 elderly students who felt that meditation led them to calm, and 1 did not.

In addition, the trainees lead the definition of happiness as calm. There were 8 students who preferred to choose a calm journey. On the contrary, the other six elderly students choose a more exciting travel journey. The results of this study showed two possibilities. One is that "meditation" can change the definition of happiness for elderly students. The other is for the temporal focus on the moment, elderly students felt more like joining a calm journey. The details are displayed in Table III.

TABLE III. MEDITATION STATISTIC TABLE

Happiness \ Journey	calm	excitement	Total
calm	7	6	13
excitement	1	0	1
Total	8	6	14

In experiment 2-2, the subjects were older and focused on the moment and defined happiness as calm. In this experiment, elder students attended the final carnival dinner and they interacted with classmates and professors during the dinner to achieve an excited mood. From the 21 questionnaires distributed, 16 were valid and 5 were invalid. The questionnaire asked "Was there excitement during the carnival dinner"?". Among the 16 valid questionnaires, all students felt that carnival dinner led them to an excited orientation. In this study, the trainees lead the definition of happiness is excitement. There are 14 old students prefer to choose a calm trip, on the contrary, the other two choose a more exciting journey.

Table IV shows the results of this study, and it showed two situations, one is the "final carnival dinner" which makes old students change the definition of happiness. Another is temporal focus which is on the moment. No matter how to guide the definition of happiness for calm or excitement, temporal focus had a more significant effect than atmosphere.

TABLE IV. FINAL CARNIVAL DINNER STATISTIC TABLE

Happiness \ Journey	calm	excitement	Total
calm	0	0	0
excitement	14	2	16
Total	14	2	16

C. Comprehensive discussion

In this experiment, we found that elderly students had a rich experience, and they were familiar with the country, language communication and even cultural differences. Those aspects maybe had a partial effect on the choice of journey. For young graduate students, any of the two journeys are the same, because both were new, so the experiment result for young graduate students was more precise than for older students.

In this study, we repeated 2x2 variance analysis and the results showed that there was a significant interaction between the "temporal focus" and "the definition of happiness" for the journey to be selected. The experiment showed graduate students' time focus on the future, and they feel more happiness from the exciting journey than the calm one. On the contrary, elderly students focus on the moment and feel more happiness from the calm journey than the exciting one. Whether the experimenter was more focused on the future or the moment, all have the probability to affect the subjects to choose either an exciting or a calm journey. Those who focus on the future are more likely to choose an exciting journey and vice versa. The final analysis explained that the choice was determined by the definition of happiness.

Specifically, the possibility of choosing an exciting journey by the experimental subjects under the temporal focus was influenced by the definition of happiness as emotional excitement. However, the possibility of choosing a calm journey by the experimental subjects under the temporal focus was influenced by the definition of happiness as emotional calm. There was a significant effect on the analysis of temporal focus, making the temporal focus on the future of the experimental subjects expected more happiness from the exciting journey. These results showed when the time was focused, the experimental subjects were expected to feel happy from the exciting and calm journey, let them to the choice of journey. Therefore, the results showed that the definition of happiness and temporal focus will affect the choice. When the desired happiness comes from the excitement of ascension, it will tend to choose an exciting option. Moreover, when the desired happiness comes from the calm of ascension, it will tend to choose a calm option.

V. CONCLUSION AND FUTURE WORK

No matter where they come from, how much money they have earned, and how old they are, people are constantly thinking about "what is the meaning of happiness?" This study began with explaining the dynamic meaning of happiness to a person, and showing how the definition of happiness naturally changes over time, and how it affects a person's decisions. In addition, the type of happiness experienced by a person may also change at a particular time, and one can choose the happiness that he or she wants to feel.

The experimental results showed that "Happiness is an option". Also, this study confirmed that the definition of happiness changes over time, and it affects the decisions of consumers. The findings in this study could help the tourism industry to analyze consumer characteristics and then provide more customized services. Furthermore, it suggests that the tourism industry can provide guidance for the consumers to choose happier journeys.

The results of this research are still tentative. In the future, we will issue more questionnaires to have holistic and persuasive results.

REFERENCES

[1] HOLA, https://www.hola.com.tw/, [last accessed June 2017].

[2] CHIMEI Group, http://www.chimei.com.tw, [last accessed June 2017].

[3] Merriam-Webster's Collegiate Dictionary, Springfield, MA: Merriam-Webster, 2009.

[4] R. Layard, "Happiness: Lessons from a New Science," New York: Penguin, 2005.

[5] D. Myers and E. Diener, "Who Is Happy?" Psychological Science, vol. 6(1), pp. 10-19, 1995.

[6] D. T. Gilbert, Stumbling on Happines. New York: Knopf, 2006.

[7] L. F. Barrett, "Discrete Emotions or Dimensions? The Role of Valence Focus and Arousal Focus," Cognition and Emotion, vol. 12(4), pp. 579-599, 1998.

[8] M. M. Bradley and P. J. Lang, "Affective Norms for English Words (ANEW): Instruction Manual and Affective Ratings," Gainesville: University of Florida Center for Research in Psychophysiology, 1999.

[9] J. Russell and L. Barrett, Core Affect, "Prototypical Emotional Episodes, and Other Things Called Emotion: Dissecting the Elephant," Journal of Personality and Social Psychology, vol. 76(5), pp. 805-819, 1999.

[10] N. Schwarz and G. L. Clors, Mood, "Misattribution, and Judgments of Well-Being: Informative and Directive Functions of Affective States," Journal of Personality and Social Psychology, vol. 45(3), pp. 512-523, 1983.

[11] A. A. Labroo and V. M. Patrick, "Providing a Moment of Respite: Why a Positive Mood Helps Seeing the Big Picture," Journal of Consumer Research, vol. 35(5), pp. 800-809, 2009.

[12] C. Mogilner, J. Aaker, and S. D. Kamvar, "How Happiness Affects Choice," Journal of Consumer Research, vol. 39, pp. 312-326, 2012.

[13] D. P. Brown and R. A. F. Thurman, "Pointing Out the Great Way: Stages of Meditation in the Mahamudra Tradition," Boston: Wisdom, 2006.

[14] E. Tolle, The Power of Now: "A Guide to Spiritual Enlightenment," Vancouver: Namaste, 1999.

Decision Making by a Fuzzy Regression Model with Modified Kernel

Kiyoshi Nagata

Faculty of Business Administration
Daito Bunka University
Tokyo 175-8571, Japan
Email: nagata@ic.daito.ac.jp

Michihiro Amagasa

Faculty of Business Administration
Hokkai Gakuen University
Sapporo 062-8605, Japan
Email: amagasa@ba.hokkai-s-u.ac.jp

***Abstract*—Regression model is a popular and powerful model for finding a rule from large amount of collected data. It is widely used in various areas for predicting the value derived from observable values. Especially in multivariate numerical analysis, several types of regression models, not only linear but also polynomial or exponential, are established. In case of non-numerical data, although fuzzy regression models are proposed and investigated by some researchers, most of them are linear models. In order to construct a non-linear regression model with fuzzy type data set, new type of devices are needed since fuzzy numbers have a complicated behavior in multiplication and division. In this paper, we try to extend a linear fuzzy regression model to non-linear model by adapting a modified kernel method.**

Keywords–Fuzzy regression model; Kernel method; Decision making.

I. INTRODUCTION

As an analysis method of numerical big-data mining, the regression model is still playing an important role. However, the huge amount of data processing requires strong computing power and resources. In particular, when handling data with non-linear features, finding a proper regression model is not easy, sometimes even infeasible. The kernel method, so-called a kernel trick, is one of smart devices solving this kind of problem. A kernel defined on the product of a data set induces an element of Hilbert space, a space of functions with an inner product, and considering a linear model in the space gives us a non-linear model in the original space. Thus, only the calculation of kernels for the given data set is non-linear, and the calculation for solving the problem to give a model is performed in the linear operation method. The kernel method is applied to many analytical systems, such as the Principal Component Analysis (PCA), [16], the Canonical Correction Analysis (CCA), [6], [12], Fisher's Linear Discriminant Analysis (LDA), [13], the Support Vector Machine(SVM), [1], [7], the regression model, [14], [17], etc.

In the real world, the collected data are sometimes expressed in linguistic values, and in order to apply well-known and authorized stochastic methods such as regression analysis, these values are transformed into numerical data. For instance, the price of a production or a service are determined from several factors, such as price of raw materials, selling expenses, consumer demand, etc. Also the price has high correlations with the customer value of product or service. Bradley T. Gale proposed a scenario where price satisfaction carries 40% of the weight and non-price attributes 60% in the customer-value equation, and showed a figure representing the relationship between relative performance overall score and relative price for luxury cars based on data [9, pp. 218-219]. In that figure, the relative price is generically expressed in linguistic values such as "Higher", "Lower", etc., then these values are transformed into numerical values in order to plot corresponding points on the performance-price plane. For the price prediction model, Inoue et al. proposed a sale price prediction model by fuzzy regression, [11], and Michihiro Amagasa, also proposed a method to handle data with uncertainty in the model of regression analysis as an extension of their model, [3]. We also give a precise formulation of a multi-variable regression model where both explanatory variables and objective one are L-R type fuzzy numbers, [4].

Construction approaches for regression models handling fuzzy set are roughly divided into two types, one is Fuzzy Least Square Regression (FLSR) and the other is dual model for possibilistic regression. The concept of FLSR model is similar to that of ordinary regression model where each value of three vertexes is processed to minimize the sum of distances between the given data and the estimated values. D'Urso adopts this approach handling linear regression model with several types of input-output data, such as crisp-fuzzy, fuzzy-crisp, and fuzzy-fuzzy, with not only type1 fuzzy data set but also type2 fuzzy data set, [8]. The dual model of possibilistic regression approach, originally proposed by Tanaka et al., [18], [19], gives upper and lower regression model by using linear programing analysis approach. Although their model is extended to non-linear models, [10], explanatory variables are still crisp values. In this paper, we propose a non-linear regression model of fuzzy input-fuzzy output type as an extension of our previously proposed model in [4] by applying the kernel method.

The rest of the paper is organized as follows: In Section II, we will review general theory of the kernel method and give a concrete construction of quadratic kernel for a small number of variables. Section III is dedicated to a brief explanation of Guo and Tanaka's non-linear fuzzy regression model and the details of our linear model. Then, in Section IV, we describe the extension version of our model into non-linear type with modified kernels. Examples to see how the proposed model works are coming up with some discussions. The last section, Section V, is the conclusion and the future works.

II. KERNEL THEORY

First, we give a brief description of kernel theory, then give an expression of the functions in the reproducing kernel Hilbert space for a quadratic kernel.

A. Overview of Kernel Theory

For any set $\mathcal{X}$ and the Hilbert space $\mathcal{H}$ of functions on $\mathcal{X}$ over $\mathbb{R}$, a positive definite kernel is a map

$$k : \mathcal{X} \times \mathcal{X} \to \mathcal{H}$$

satisfying

- $k(x, y) = k(y, x)$ for any $x, y \in \mathcal{X}$,
- For any $\{c_i\} \subset \mathbb{R}$ and any $\{x_i\} \subset \mathcal{X}$,

$$\sum c_i c_j k(x_i, x_j) \geq 0.$$

Here, we give some examples of kernel over $\mathbb{R}^k$.
For $\vec{x} = (x_1, \ldots, x_k), \vec{y} = (y_1, \ldots, y_k)$,

- $k(\vec{x}, \vec{y}) = \vec{x}^t \vec{y} = \sum_{i=1}^k x_i y_i$ (linear kernel)
- $k_P(\vec{x}, \vec{y}) = (\vec{x}^t \vec{y} + c)^d$, with $c \geq 0$, $0 < d \in \mathbb{Z}$ (polynomial kernel)
- $k_E(\vec{x}, \vec{y}) = exp(\beta \vec{x}^t \vec{y})$, with $\beta > 0$ (exponential kernel)
- $k_G(\vec{x}, \vec{y}) = exp(-\frac{1}{2\sigma^2}\|\vec{x} - \vec{y}\|^2)$ (Gaussian radial basis function kernel)
- $k_L(\vec{x}, \vec{y}) = exp(-\alpha \sum_{i=1}^k |x_i - y_i|)$ (Laplacian kernel)

If, for any $x \in \mathcal{X}$, there exists a function $k_x \in \mathcal{H}$ such that

$$f(x) = < f, k_x >_{\mathcal{H}}, (\forall f \in \mathcal{H}) \tag{1}$$

where $< \cdot, \cdot >_{\mathcal{H}}$ is the inner product of the Hilbert space, the Hilbert space $\mathcal{H}$ is called a Reproducing Kernel Hilbert Space (RKHS). It is shown that $k_x \in \mathcal{H}$ is unique, and $k(\cdot, x) = k_x$ is a positive definite kernel on $\mathcal{X}$ called the reproducing kernel.

Conversely, the following theorem is known, [5].

Theorem 1. *(Moore-Aronszajn) For any positive definite kernel on $\mathcal{X}$, there exist unique Hilbert space $\mathcal{H}$ satisfying*

1) $k(\cdot, x) \in \mathcal{H}$ (for any $x \in \mathcal{X}$),

2) The subspace spanned by $\{k(\cdot, x); x \in \mathcal{X}\}$ is dense in $\mathcal{H}$,

3) k is the reproducing kernel of $\mathcal{H}$.

Although Hilbert space has infinity dimension, solution of some optimization problem with data, if there is any, can be expressed as a linear combination of at most the number of data elements in $\mathcal{H}$. This is guaranteed by the following theorem, [15].

Theorem 2. *(The Representer Theorem) Let k be a kernel on $\mathcal{X}$ and let $\mathcal{H}$ be its associated RKHS. Fix $x_1, \cdots, x_n \in \mathcal{X}$, and consider the optimization problem*

$$\min_{f \in \mathcal{H}} D(f(x_1), \ldots, f(x_n)) + P(\|f\|^2_{\mathcal{H}}) \tag{2}$$

where P is nondecreasing and D depends only on $f(x_1), \cdots, f(x_n)$. If there is a minimizer, then it has the form of

$$f = \sum_{i=1}^n a_i k(\cdot, x_i) \tag{3}$$

with some $a_1, \cdots, a_n \in \mathbb{R}$. Furthermore, if P is strictly increasing, then every solution has this form.

B. Example Expression of RKHS Basis

From the representer theorem, we can express an optimal function as in the form of (3). However, if the given data set is big, we will have many unknown variables $\{a_i\}_{i=1,\ldots,n}$ to be determined. For the convenience of calculation, we try to reduce the number of components for the polynomial kernel and give an example for the quadratic polynomial kernel of the case that $d = 2$ and $k = 3$ variables.

From the representer theorem and the equation below,

$$k_P(\vec{x}, \vec{y}) = (\textstyle\sum_{j=1}^k x_j y_j + c)^d = \sum_{\substack{0 \leq e_1 + \cdots + e_k \leq d \\ 0 \leq e_j}} c^{d-(e_1+\cdot+e_k)} x_1^{e_1} \cdots x_k^{e_k} y_1^{e_1} \cdots y_k^{e_k}$$

we have that for any $(e_1, \ldots, e_k)$ such that $0 \leq e_1 + \cdots + e_k \leq d, 0 \leq e_i$, there exist $N =_{k+d} C_d$ vectors, $\vec{x}_1, \ldots \vec{x}_N$, and $a_1, \ldots, a_N$ satisfying

$$\sum_{i=1}^N a_i x_{i1}^{f_1} \cdots x_{ik}^{f_k} = \begin{cases} c^{-(d-(e_1+\cdot+e_k))} & \text{if}(f_1 \ldots, f_k) = (e_1, \ldots, e_k), \\ 0 & \text{otherwise.} \end{cases} \tag{4}$$

In a simple case of $d = 2$ and $k = 3$ then $N =_5 C_2 = 10$, and the left side of equation (4) is expressed as

$$\begin{pmatrix} x_{11}^2 & x_{21}^2 & \cdots & x_{10\,1}^2 \\ x_{12}^2 & x_{22}^2 & \cdots & x_{10\,2}^2 \\ x_{13}^2 & x_{23}^2 & \cdots & x_{10\,3}^2 \\ x_{11} & x_{21} & \cdots & x_{10\,1} \\ x_{12} & x_{22} & \cdots & x_{10\,2} \\ x_{13} & x_{23} & \cdots & x_{10\,3} \\ x_{11}x_{12} & x_{21}x_{22} & \cdots & x_{10\,1}x_{10\,2} \\ x_{11}x_{13} & x_{21}x_{23} & \cdots & x_{10\,1}x_{10\,3} \\ x_{12}x_{13} & x_{22}x_{23} & \cdots & x_{10\,2}x_{10\,3} \\ 1 & 1 & \cdots & 1 \end{pmatrix} \begin{pmatrix} a_1 \\ a_2 \\ \vdots \\ \vdots \\ a_{10} \end{pmatrix}.$$

However, we only have to determine $\vec{x}_1, \vec{x}_2, \vec{x}_3$ and solve the 10 equations of (4) shown as follows.

$$\begin{pmatrix} x_{1j}^2 & x_{2j}^2 & x_{3j}^2 \\ x_{1j} & x_{2j} & x_{3j} \\ 1 & 1 & 1 \end{pmatrix} \begin{pmatrix} a_1 \\ a_2 \\ a_3 \end{pmatrix} = \begin{pmatrix} 1 \\ 0 \\ 0 \end{pmatrix}, \begin{pmatrix} 0 \\ c \\ 0 \end{pmatrix}, \begin{pmatrix} 0 \\ 0 \\ c^2 \end{pmatrix},$$

or

$$\begin{pmatrix} x_{1j}^2 & x_{2j}^2 & x_{3j}^2 \\ x_{1j} & x_{2j} & x_{3j} \\ x_{1j}x_{1l} & x_{2j}x_{2l} & x_{3j}x_{3l} \end{pmatrix} \begin{pmatrix} a_1 \\ a_2 \\ a_3 \end{pmatrix} = \begin{pmatrix} 0 \\ 0 \\ 1 \end{pmatrix},$$

where $j, l = 1, 2, 3$ and $j \neq l$. Just analyzing the invertibility of these matrices, we have 10 functions spanning the dense subspace $\mathcal{H}'_k$ of $\mathcal{H}_k$.

$$\mathcal{H}'_k = < k(\cdot, \vec{x}_i); i = 1, \ldots, 10 >_{\mathbb{R}},$$

where
$\vec{x}_1 = (1, 0, 0)$, $\vec{x}_2 = (0, 1, 0)$, $\vec{x}_3 = (0, 0, 1)$,
$\vec{x}_4 = (-1, 0, 0)$, $\vec{x}_5 = (0, -1, 0)$, $\vec{x}_6 = (0, 0, -1)$,
$\vec{x}_7 = (1, 1, 0)$, $\vec{x}_8 = (0, 1, 1)$, $\vec{x}_9 = (1, 0, 1)$, and
$\vec{x}_{10} = (0, 0, 0)$.

III. Some Existing Fuzzy Regression Model

In this section, we will give a brief explanation of two fuzzy regression models, one is crisp-input and fuzzy-output type by Guo and Tanaka, and the other is fuzzy-input and fuzzy-output type.

A. Guo and Tanaka's Non-Linear Model

Guo and Tanaka have investigated the dual possibilistic regression models of both linear and non-linear types with crisp-input and symmetric triangular fuzzy-output in [10]. At first, the linear model whose output $Y = (y;p)_F = (y;p,p)_F$ from crisp input values for variables x_j $(j = 1,\ldots,k)$ is defined as follows,

$$Y = A_1x_1 + A_2x_2 + \cdots + A_kx_k, \tag{5}$$

with symmetric fuzzy coefficients $A_j = (a_j;r_j)_F$ $(j = 1,\ldots,k)$. In this formula, the value of Y is obtained by calculating $(\sum_{j=1}^k a_jc_j, \sum_{j=1}^k r_j|c_j|)$, once explicit values $c_1,\ldots,c_k$ for each given variable. When we have a data set of n number of data, $\{(Y_i;x_{i1},\cdots,x_{ik})\}_{i=1,\ldots,n}$ with crisp x_{ij} and symmetric fuzzy numbers $Y_i = (y_i;p_i)_F$, we consider the upper regression model and the lower regression model.

For the upper regression model, try to find fuzzy coefficients $A_j^* = (a_j^*;r_j^*)_F$ such that

$$\begin{array}{l}\text{Minimizing: } J(\vec{r^*}) = \sum_{j=1}^k r_j^*\left(\sum_{i=1}^n |x_{ij}|\right),\\ \text{under the condition}\\ Y_i \subseteq Y_i^* = A_1^*x_{i1} + \cdots + A_k^*x_{ik} \qquad (i = 1,\ldots,n).\end{array} \tag{6}$$

The inclusion condition above can be expressed by the following equations, because the shapes of fuzzy set are supposed to be similar

$$\begin{cases} y_i - p_i \geq \sum_{j=1}^k a_j^*x_{ij} - \sum_{j=1}^k r_j^*|x_{ij}| \\ y_i + p_i \leq \sum_{j=1}^k a_j^*x_{ij} + \sum_{j=1}^k r_j^*|x_{ij}| \\ r_j^* \geq 0 \end{cases}. \tag{7}$$

For the lower regression model, try to find fuzzy coefficients $A_{j*} = (a_{j*};r_{j*})_F$ such that

$$\begin{array}{l}\text{Maximizing: } J(\vec{r_*}) = \sum_{j=1}^k r_{j*}\left(\sum_{i=1}^n |x_{ij}|\right),\\ \text{under the condition}\\ Y_i \supseteq Y_{i*} = A_{1*}x_{i1} + \cdots + A_{k*}x_{ik} \qquad (i = 1,\ldots,n).\end{array} \tag{8}$$

The inclusion condition above also can be expressed by the following equations.

$$\begin{cases} y_i - p_i \leq \sum_{j=1}^k a_{j*}x_{ij} - \sum_{j=1}^k r_{j*}|x_{ij}| \\ y_i + p_i \geq \sum_{j=1}^k a_{j*}x_{ij} + \sum_{j=1}^k r_{j*}|x_{ij}| \\ r_{j*} \geq 0 \end{cases}. \tag{9}$$

For the existence of upper and lower regression model, Guo and Tanaka showed the following theorem.

Theorem 3. *(by Guo and Tanaka, [10])*

1) *There always exists an optimal solution in the upper regression model (6) under (7).*
2) *There exists an optimal solution in the lower regression model (8) under (9) if and only if there exist $a_{1*}^{(0)}, a_{2*}^{(0)}, \ldots, a_{k*}^{(0)}$ satisfying*

$$y_i - p_i \leq \sum_{j=1}^k a_{j*}^{(0)}x_{ij} \leq y_i + p_i \qquad (i = 1,\ldots,n). \tag{10}$$

From the theorem, there might not be any optimal solution for the lower regression model. This problem is caused by the relationship between the number of variables and the number of data. They tried to solve the problems by extending the model into non-linear model which has more formal variables x_ix_j $(i,j = 1,\ldots,k)$ in the following formula.

$$Y = A_0 + \sum_{j=1}^k A_jx_j + \sum_{j,l=1}^k A_{jl}x_jx_l, \tag{11}$$

with symmetric fuzzy coefficients A_j, A_{jl} $(j,l = 1,\ldots,k)$. The right hand side has a quadratic part when considering x_i variables, however we need to find A_j and A_{jl} for a given data set which minimize or maximize the value, so this might be solved by LP method.

B. Our Linear Model

As a general type of fuzzy number, we consider L-R fuzzy set with monotone decreasing functions satisfying $L(0) = R(0) = 1$ and $L(1) = R(1) = 0$, and denote a L-R fuzzy set by $Y = (y;p,q)_F$, where y is the value giving the maximum uncertainty, e.g., 1, and p, q are left and right range from y, i.e., $y-p$ and $y+q$ give the uncertainty value 0, [2]. We proposed the following type of possibilistic fuzzy regression model

$$Y = A_1X_1 + A_2X_2 + \cdots + A_kX_k, \tag{12}$$

with L-R fuzzy variables $Y = (y;p,q)_F$ and $X_j = (x_j;w_j,z_j)_F$ and L-R fuzzy coefficients $A_j = (a_j;r_j,s_j)_F$ $(j = 1,\ldots,k)$.

Let $[Y]_h$ be the support of fuzzy number Y above h-cut line, we have

$$\begin{array}{l}[Y]_h = [y - pL^{-1}(h), y + qR^{-1}(h)],\\ [X_j]_h = [x_j - w_jL^{-1}(h), x_j + z_jR^{-1}(h)],\\ [A_j]_h = [a_j - r_jL^{-1}(h), a_j + s_jR^{-1}(h)].\end{array}$$

Applying commonly known multiplication and summation of L-R fuzzy numbers, we have

$$\begin{aligned}[\textstyle\sum_{j=1}^k A_jX_j]_h = & [\textstyle\sum_{j=1}^k(a_j - r_jL^{-1}(h))(x_j - w_jL^{-1}(h)),\\ & \textstyle\sum_{j=1}^k(a_j + s_jR^{-1}(h))(x_j + z_jR^{-1}(h))]_h,\end{aligned}$$

and the range of the interval, denoted by J, is calculated by subtracting the left end value from the right end value. Then

$$\begin{aligned}J = & \textstyle\sum_{j=1}^k\{(z_jR^{-1}(h) + w_jL^{-1}(h))a_j\\ & +(x_j + z_jR^{-1}(h))R^{-1}(h)s_j\\ & +(x_j - w_jL^{-1}(h))L^{-1}(h)r_j\}.\end{aligned}$$

Following Guo and Tanaka, we consider upper and lower models, and describe the inclusion relation of the support of Y_i and that of the obtained fuzzy number in the regression model for a given data set.

Now we let ZW_j, XZ_j, XW_j be as follows,

$$\begin{cases} ZW_j = (\sum_{i=1}^n z_{ij})R^{-1}(h) + (\sum_{i=1}^n w_{ij})L^{-1}(h) \\ XZ_j = ((\sum_{i=1}^n x_{ij}) + (\sum_{i=1}^n z_{ij})R^{-1}(h))R^{-1}(h) \\ XW_j = ((\sum_{i=1}^n x_{ij}) - (\sum_{i=1}^n w_{ij})L^{-1}(h))L^{-1}(h) \end{cases}. \tag{13}$$

Then our upper model Y^* is constructed with $A_j^* = (a_j^*;r_j^*,s_j^*)_F$, such that

$$\begin{array}{l}\text{Minimizing: } J(\mathbb{A}^*) = \sum_{j=1}^k(ZW_ja_j^* + XZ_js_j^* + XW_jr_j^*),\\ \text{where } \mathbb{A}^* = (A_1^*,\ldots,A_k^*),\end{array} \tag{14}$$

under the condition that for all i

$$\begin{cases} y_i - p_i L^{-1}(h) \geq \sum_{j=1}^{k}(a_j^* - r_j^* L^{-1}(h))\times \\ \qquad (x_{ij} - w_{ij}L^{-1}(h)) \\ y_i + q_i R^{-1}(h) \leq \sum_{j=1}^{k}(a_j^* + s_j^* R^{-1}(h))\times \\ \qquad (x_{ij} + z_{ij}R^{-1}(h)) \\ r_j^*,\ s_j^* \geq 0 \end{cases} . \tag{15}$$

The lower model Y_* is similarly constructed with $A_{j*} = (a_{j*}; r_{j*}, s_{j*})_F$, such that

$$\text{Maximizing: } J(\mathbb{A}_*) = \sum_{j=1}^{k}(ZW_j a_{j*} + XZ_j s_{j*} + XW_j r_{j*}), \text{ where } \mathbb{A}_* = (A_{1*}, \ldots, A_{k*}), \tag{16}$$

under the condition that for all i

$$\begin{cases} y_i - p_i L^{-1}(h) \leq \sum_{j=1}^{k}(a_{j*} - r_{j*} L^{-1}(h))\times \\ \qquad (x_{ij} - w_{ij}L^{-1}(h)) \\ y_i + q_i R^{-1}(h) \geq \sum_{j=1}^{k}(a_{j*} + s_{j*} R^{-1}(h))\times \\ \qquad (x_{ij} + z_{ij}R^{-1}(h)) \\ r_{j*},\ s_{j*} \geq 0 \end{cases} . \tag{17}$$

We could also show the following theorem similar to the Theorem 3 on the existence of models.

Theorem 4. *When $x_{ij} - w_{ij}L^{-1}(h) > 0$ $(i = 1, \ldots, n,\ j = 1, \ldots, k)$, then*

1) *There always exists an optimal solution in the upper regression model (14) under (15) .*
2) *There exists an optimal solution in the lower regression model (16) under (17) if and only if there exist $a_{1*}^{(0)}, a_{2*}^{(0)}, \ldots, a_{k*}^{(0)}$ satisfying*

$$\begin{cases} y_i - p_i L^{-1}(h) \leq \sum_{j=1}^{k}(x_{ij} - w_{ij}L^{-1}(h))a_{j*}^{(0)} \\ y_i + q_i R^{-1}(h) \geq \sum_{j=1}^{k}(x_{ij} + z_{ij}R^{-1}(h))a_{j*}^{(0)} \end{cases} . \tag{18}$$

Proof.

1) If $x_{ij} - w_{ij}L^{-1}(h) \geq 0$ in (15), then $x_{ij} > 0$ from $w_{ij} \geq 0$ and $0 \leq L^{-1}(h) \leq 1$. Therefore $x_{ij} + z_{ij}R^{-1}(h)$ are also non-negative, and sufficiently large r_j^* and s_j^* satisfy the condition.
2) If there exist $A_{j*} = (a_{j*}; r_{j*}, s_{j*})_F$ $(j = 1, \ldots, k)$ satisfying (17), then we have the condition (18). Conversely, for $a_{j*}^{(0)}$ satisfying (18), put $A_{j*}^{(0)} = (a_{j*}^{(0)}; 0, 0)_F$ and they satisfy the condition (17).

□

Remark1: When the data for independent variables are given in linguistic values, they are usually transformed into fuzzy numbers satisfying the condition $x_{ij} - w_{ij}L^{-1}(h) > 0$ $(i = 1, \ldots, n,\ j = 1, \ldots, k)$. So, the assumptions in the Theorem 4 are not special condition.

Remark2: The condition (18) means the inclusion relation between Y_i and the resulted fuzzy number Y_{i*} of areas between h-cut horizontal line and the base-line ($h = 0$) of them.

Remark2.1: In case of $h = 1$, $L^{-1}(1) = R^{-1}(1) = 0$ and (18) is reduced to

$$y_i = \sum_{j=1}^{k} x_{ij} a_{j*}^{(0)},$$

which means that the line segment of Y_{i*} is in the area of Y_i.

Remark2.2: In case of $h = 0$, $L^{-1}(0) = R^{-1}(0) = 1$ and (18) is reduced to

$$\begin{cases} y_i - p_i \leq \sum_{j=1}^{k}(x_{ij} - w_{ij})a_{j*}^{(0)} \leq \sum_{j=1}^{k} x_{ij}a_{j*}^{(0)} \\ y_i + q_i \geq \sum_{j=1}^{k}(x_{ij} + z_{ij})a_{j*}^{(0)} \geq \sum_{j=1}^{k} x_{ij}a_{j*}^{(0)} \end{cases} .$$

which means that $Y_{i*} \cap Y_i \neq \phi$.

IV. Regression Method with Kernel

We extend our linear model to a regression model with a kernel-like function, we call modified kernel, on a set of L-R fuzzy number. First we describe a general formula, then give more precise formula as an extension of the polynomial kernel, $k_P(x, y)$, for the case of degree $d = 2$ and the number of explanatory variables $k = 3$ as described in B. of section II.

A. General Formula

We suppose that there exists a function $K(X, Y)$ satisfying only $K(Y, X) = K(X, Y)$ on the product of a set of fuzzy numbers, $\mathcal{X}_F^k \times \mathcal{X}_F^k$ to $\mathcal{X}_F$. Actually, we use a function induced from one of kernels explained in A. of section II if it can be well-defined on fuzzy numbers.

For a given data set of L-R fuzzy numbers, $\{(Y_i, \mathbb{X}_i); i = 1, \ldots, M\}$, where $Y_i = (y_i; p_i, q_i)_F$, $\mathbb{X}_i = (X_{i1}, \ldots X_{ik})_F$ with $X_{ij} = (x_{ij}; w_{ij}, z_{ij})_F$ $(i = 1, \ldots, M, j = 1, \ldots, k)$. We just modify the formula (12) by replacing X_j with $K(\mathbb{X}, \mathbb{X}_i)$, and consider the model

$$Y = A_1K(\mathbb{X}, \mathbb{X}_1) + A_2K(\mathbb{X}, \mathbb{X}_2) + \cdots + A_MK(\mathbb{X}, \mathbb{X}_M), \tag{19}$$

where $\mathbb{X} = (X_1, \ldots, X_k)$ is vector expression of the explanation fuzzy variable and Y is the objective fuzzy variable. For this formula, we can apply our proposed method for the dual model with h-cut. Since the number of data, M, is usually much greater than the number of explanatory variables, k, the possibility of existence for the lower model increases from the Theorem 4.

On the other hand, when M is very big, there will be too many possible fuzzy number coefficients $\{A_i\}$ for both upper and lower model. Thus, try to find smaller set of representer if possible, and denote their number by N. Then fuzzy coefficients $\mathbb{A}^* = (A_1^*, \ldots, A_N^*)$ and $\mathbb{A}_* = (A_{1*}, \ldots, A_{N*})$ are calculated for upper and lower models from the following formulas of fuzzy numbers respectively,

$$A_1K(\mathbb{X}_i, \tilde{\mathbb{X}}_1) + A_2K(\mathbb{X}_i, \tilde{\mathbb{X}}_2) + \cdots + A_NK(\mathbb{X}_i, \tilde{\mathbb{X}}_N), \tag{20}$$

where $i = 1, \ldots, M$, and $\{\tilde{\mathbb{X}}_l; l = 1, \ldots, N\}$ is a representer.

B. Case of Modified Polynomial Kernel

Here we consider a modified kernel induced from polynomial kernel, $k_P(x, y)$, denoted by $K_F(\mathbb{X}, \tilde{\mathbb{X}}) = (\mathbb{X}^t\tilde{\mathbb{X}} + C)^d$. When we could find $N(={}_{k+d}C_d)$ number of proper value vectors $\vec{\tilde{x}}_l = (\tilde{x}_{l1}, \ldots, \tilde{x}_{lk})$ $(l = 1, \ldots, N)$ for the dense subspace of $\mathcal{H}_{k_P}$, put $\tilde{\mathbb{X}}_l = (\tilde{X}_{l1}, \ldots, \tilde{X}_{lk})$ with $\tilde{X}_{li} = (\tilde{x}_{li}; 0, 0)_F$ $(l = 1, \ldots, N)$.

Now calculate the h-cut of the equation (20) for $C = (c; 0, 0)_F$ in the way of B. of section III. When putting $\vec{x}_i =$

$(x_{i1}, \ldots, x_{ik})$, $\vec{w}_i = (w_{i1}, \ldots, w_{ik})$, $\vec{z}_i = (z_{i1}, \ldots, z_{ik})$, $i = 1, \ldots, M$,we have

$$[\mathbb{X}_i]_h = ([X_{i1}]_h, \ldots, [X_{ik}]_h) = [\vec{x}_i - L^{-1}(h)\vec{w}_i, \vec{x}_i + R^{-1}(h)\vec{z}_i],$$

and the h-cut of the modified kernel is as follows,

$$\begin{aligned}
[K(\mathbb{X}_i, \tilde{\mathbb{X}}_l)]_h &= \left(\textstyle\sum_j^k [X_{ij}]_h [\tilde{X}_{lj}]_h + [C]_h\right)^d \\
&= \left[\left(\textstyle\sum_{j=1}^k (x_{ij} - w_{ij}L^{-1}(h))\tilde{x}_{lj} + c\right)^d,\right. \\
&\qquad \left.\left(\textstyle\sum_{j=1}^k (x_{ij} + z_{ij}R^{-1}(h))\tilde{x}_{lj} + c\right)^d\right] \\
&= \left[k_P(\vec{x}_i - L^{-1}(h)\vec{w}_i, \vec{\tilde{x}}_l), k_P(\vec{x}_i + R^{-1}(h)\vec{z}_i, \vec{\tilde{x}}_l)\right].
\end{aligned}$$

Thus we have

$$\begin{aligned}
&\left[\sum_{l=1}^N A_l K(\mathbb{X}_i, \tilde{\mathbb{X}}_l)\right]_h \\
&= \left[\sum_{l=1}^N (a_l - r_l L^{-1}(h)) k_P(\vec{x}_i - L^{-1}(h)\vec{w}_i, \vec{\tilde{x}}_l),\right. \qquad (21) \\
&\qquad \left.\sum_{l=1}^N (a_l + s_l R^{-1}(h)) k_P(\vec{x}_i + R^{-1}(h)\vec{z}_i, \vec{\tilde{x}}_l)\right],
\end{aligned}$$

and minimizing or maximizing objective value is

$$\begin{aligned}
J(\mathbb{A}) = \sum_{l=1}^N a_l &\left(\tfrac{1}{M}\textstyle\sum_{i=1}^M \left(k_P(\vec{x}_i + R^{-1}(h)\vec{z}_i, \vec{\tilde{x}}_l)\right.\right. \\
&\qquad \left.\left. - k_P(\vec{x}_i - L^{-1}(h)\vec{w}_i, \vec{\tilde{x}}_l)\right)\right) \\
&+ R^{-1}(h) \sum_{l=1}^N s_l \tfrac{1}{M} \textstyle\sum_{i=1}^M k_P(\vec{x}_i + R^{-1}(h)\vec{z}_i, \vec{\tilde{x}}_l) \\
&+ L^{-1}(h) \sum_{l=1}^N r_l \tfrac{1}{M} \textstyle\sum_{i=1}^M k_P(\vec{x}_i - L^{-1}(h)\vec{w}_i, \vec{\tilde{x}}_l),
\end{aligned} \tag{22}$$

where $\vec{\tilde{x}}_l = (\tilde{x}_{l1}, \ldots, \tilde{x}_{lk})$ for $l = 1, \ldots, N$.

Then our upper model Y^* is constructed with $A_j^* = (a_j^*; r_j^*, s_j^*)_F$ minimizing $J(\mathbb{A}^*)$ under the condition that for all $i = 1, \ldots, M$,

$$\left\{\begin{array}{l}
y_i - p_i L^{-1}(h) \geq \sum_{l=1}^N (a_l^* - r_l^* L^{-1}(h)) \times \\
\qquad\qquad k_P(\vec{x}_i - L^{-1}(h)\vec{w}_i, \vec{\tilde{x}}_l) \\
y_i + q_i R^{-1}(h) \leq \sum_{l=1}^N (a_l^* + s_l^* R^{-1}(h)) \times \\
\qquad\qquad k_P(\vec{x}_i + R^{-1}(h)\vec{z}_i, \vec{\tilde{x}}_l) \\
r_j^*,\ s_j^* \geq 0
\end{array}\right. . \tag{23}$$

The lower model Y_* is similarly constructed with $A_{j*} = (a_{j*}; r_{j*}, s_{j*})_F$ maximizing $J(\mathbb{A}_*)$ under the condition that for all $i = 1, \ldots, M$,

$$\left\{\begin{array}{l}
y_i - p_i L^{-1}(h) \leq \sum_{l=1}^N (a_{l*} - r_{l*} L^{-1}(h)) \times \\
\qquad\qquad k_P(\vec{x}_i - L^{-1}(h)\vec{w}_i, \vec{\tilde{x}}_l) \\
y_i + q_i R^{-1}(h) \geq \sum_{l=1}^N (a_{l*} + s_* l R^{-1}(h)) \times \\
\qquad\qquad k_P(\vec{x}_i + R^{-1}(h)\vec{z}_i, \vec{\tilde{x}}_l) \\
r_{j*},\ s_{j*} \geq 0
\end{array}\right. . \tag{24}$$

We also have the same kind of theorem as Theorem 4.

Theorem 5. *When $k_P(\vec{x}_i - L^{-1}(h)\vec{w}_i, \vec{\tilde{x}}_l) > 0$ and $k_P(\vec{x}_i + R^{-1}(h)\vec{z}_i, \vec{\tilde{x}}_l) > 0$ $(i = 1, \ldots, M,\ l = 1, \ldots, N)$, then*

1) *There always exists an optimal solution in the upper regression model under (23) .*
2) *There exists an optimal solution in the lower regression model under (24) if and only if there exist $a_{1*}^{(0)}, \ldots, a_{N*}^{(0)}$ satisfying*

$$\left\{\begin{array}{l}
y_i - p_i L^{-1}(h) \leq \sum_{l=1}^N k_P(\vec{x}_i - L^{-1}(h)\vec{w}_i, \vec{\tilde{x}}_l) a_{l*}^{(0)} \\
y_i + q_i R^{-1}(h) \geq \sum_{l=1}^N k_P(\vec{x}_i + R^{-1}(h)\vec{z}_i, \vec{\tilde{x}}_l) a_{l*}^{(0)}
\end{array}\right. . \tag{25}$$

C. Illustrative Example

As an illustrative example, we consider a polynomial kernel $k_P(x, y)$ of degree $d = 2$ and the number of explanatory variables $k = 3$ cases, so the number of basis for the dense subspace $\mathcal{H}'_k$ of $\mathcal{H}_k$ is $N = 10$. Only considering triangular type fuzzy numbers, i. e., $L = R$ is the linear function from $(0, 1)$ to $(1, 0)$ and $L^{-1}(h) = R^{-1}(h) = 1 - h$, and using the base vectors given in B. of section II, we have

$$\begin{array}{l}
\tilde{\mathbb{X}}_l = (\tilde{X}_{l1}, \tilde{X}_{l2}, \tilde{X}_{l3}) \quad (l = 1, \ldots, 10) \text{ with} \\
\tilde{X}_{11} = (1; 0, 0)_F, \tilde{X}_{22} = (1; 0, 0)_F, \tilde{X}_{33} = (1; 0, 0)_F, \\
\tilde{X}_{41} = (-1; 0, 0)_F, \tilde{X}_{52} = (-1; 0, 0)_F, \tilde{X}_{63} = (-1; 0, 0)_F, \\
\tilde{X}_{71} = (1; 0, 0)_F, \tilde{X}_{72} = (1; 0, 0)_F, \\
\tilde{X}_{82} = (1; 0, 0)_F, \tilde{X}_{83} = (1; 0, 0)_F, \\
\tilde{X}_{91} = (1; 0, 0)_F, \tilde{X}_{93} = (1; 0, 0)_F, \\
\tilde{X}_{lj} = (0; , 0, 0)_F \quad \text{otherwise.}
\end{array}$$

Here, we have $M = 8$ pairs of fuzzy numbers as an example data set shown in Table I. From these fuzzy numbers, calculate $k_P(\vec{x}_i - L^{-1}(h)\vec{w}_i, \vec{\tilde{x}}_l)$ and $k_P(\vec{x}_i + R^{-1}(h)\vec{z}_i, \vec{\tilde{x}}_l)$ for each pair of (i, l) $(i = 1, \ldots, 8,\ l = 1, \ldots, 10)$, then take averages through i for each l. Notice that the calculation is done using $\vec{\tilde{x}}_l$ not $\tilde{X}_{l,i}$.

Next, after setting the constant value for c and the value for h-cut, solve two LP problems, one is for upper model with $\mathbb{A}^*$ and the other is lower model with $\mathbb{A}_*$, satisfying the conditions (23) and (24) respectively.

TABLE I. DATA SET FOR THE ILLUSTRATIVE EXAMPLE

$(y; p, q)_F$	$(x_1; w_1, z_1)_F$	$(x_2; w_2, z_2)_F$	$(x_3; w_3, z_3)_F$
$(3.5; 1.5, 1.5)$	$(1.0; 0.5, 0.1)$	$(2.0; 0.5, 0.5)$	$(3.0; 0.5, 1.0)$
$(4.5; 2.0, 2.0)$	$(2.0; 0.5, 0.1)$	$(2.0; 0.5, 1.0)$	$(3.5; 0.75, 1.0)$
$(7.0; 2.5, 2.5)$	$(3.0; 0.1, 0.0)$	$(6.5; 0.5, 1.5)$	$(5.5; 1.0, 1.25)$
$(9.5; 2.0, 2.0)$	$(2.0; 0.5, 0.1)$	$(9.5; 1.0, 0.5)$	$(10.0; 2.0, 2.5)$
$(11.0; 3.0, 3.0)$	$(4.0; 0.5, 1.0)$	$(9.0; 1.0, 1.0)$	$(10.5; 3.0, 2.5)$
$(6.0; 2.0, 2.0)$	$(2.0; 0.0, 0.0)$	$(3.0; 1.0, 2.0)$	$(2.0; 0.5, 1.0)$
$(8.0; 2.5, 2.5)$	$(3.0; 0.1, 0.0)$	$(5.0; 1.5, 1.5)$	$(5.0; 1.5, 2.0)$
$(9.0; 3.0, 3.0)$	$(3.5; 0.5, 0.0)$	$(4.0; 0.5, 0.5)$	$(6.0; 2.0, 1.25)$

By applying the solver function in MS-EXCEL, when setting $c = 1$ and $h = 0.3$, for the upper model we have

$$\begin{array}{l}
A_1^* = (0.218; 0, 0.038)_F, A_6^* = (0.030; 0, 0)_F, \\
A_{10}^* = (1.455; 0, 5.230)_F, A_l^* = (0; 0, 0)_F \quad \text{(for other } l\text{)},
\end{array}$$

and

$$Y = A_1^* K(\mathbb{X}, \tilde{\mathbb{X}}_1) + A_6^* K(\mathbb{X}, \tilde{\mathbb{X}}_6) + A_{10}^* K(\mathbb{X}, \tilde{\mathbb{X}}_{10}). \tag{26}$$

For the lower model, we have

$$A_{1*} = (0.160; 0, 0.038)_F, A_{2*} = (0.037; 0, 0)_F,$$
$$A_{3*} = (0.002; 0, 0)_F, A_{10*} = (3.301; 0, 0.167)_F,$$
$$A_{l*} = (0; 0, 0)_F \quad \text{(for other } l\text{)},$$

and

$$Y = A_{1*}K(\mathbb{X}, \tilde{\mathbb{X}}_1) + A_{2*}K(\mathbb{X}, \tilde{\mathbb{X}}_2) + A_{3*}K(\mathbb{X}, \tilde{\mathbb{X}}_3) + A_{10*}K(\mathbb{X}, \tilde{\mathbb{X}}_{10}). \quad (27)$$

Table II describes the correspondence of original values and the resulted values by lower model (27) and by upper model (26). The expression of fuzzy numbers here is not the same as used so far in this paper. These values express the left edge, the center point, and the right edge of each triangular shape. We can see three corresponding fuzzy numbers have no inclusion relation, because they are full numbers before operating h-cut procedure. When looking at the support interval of h-cut of each fuzzy set, we have the set relationship $[Y_*]_h \subset [Y]_h \subset [Y^*]_h$. Figure 1 illustrates the relationship among three fuzzy numbers from the second row in Table II.

TABLE II. COMPARISON: Y, Y^*, AND Y_*

$(y-p, y, y+q)$	(y^*-p^*, y^*, y^*+q^*)	(y_*-p_*, y_*, y_*+q_2)
(2.0, 3.5, 5.0)	(2.0, 2.4, 8.1)	(3.9, 4.3, 4.8)
(2.5, 4.5, 6.5)	(2.9, 3.6, 9.5)	(4.6, 5.1, 6.0)
(4.5, 7.0, 9.5)	(5.1, 5.6, 11.8)	(7.6, 8.0, 9.8)
(7.5, 9.5, 11.5)	(4.3, 5.8, 13.1)	(7.8, 9.1, 10.2)
(8.0, 11.0, 14.0)	(7.1, 9.6, 20.2)	(9.7, 11.3, 15.5)
(4.0, 6.0, 8.0)	(3.4, 3.4, 9.1)	(5.1, 5.4, 6.6)
(5.5, 8.0, 10.5)	(5.0, 5.4, 11.9)	(6.5, 7.3, 8.8)
(6.0, 9.0, 12.0)	(5.2, 6.6, 13.0)	(6.7, 7.6, 8.7)

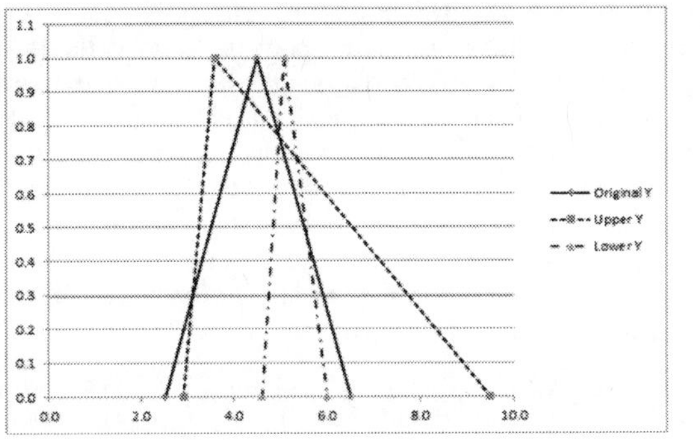

Figure 1. Relationship of Three Fuzzy Numbers

We also tried other type of kernels for these test data, and may have some discussion on the fitness.

V. CONCLUSION

As an extension of our fuzzy dual linear regression model, we proposed to apply kernel method and give a general formula with a modified kernel of polynomial type. Then, we showed how it works using artificial sample data set for illustration of performance in a simple case.

Although we could see that the kernel method can be incorporated with fuzzy regression model, the effectiveness of our method, depending on data set type, is not yet clear. In the example handling small data, when changing the values slightly, we could not have any solution for the lower model. This infeasibility also occurs by increasing the value of h, which may reduce the degree of freedom of resulted fuzzy number of lower model. Though the number of data is less than the number of base set, the merit of choosing base set is that the number N depends only on the degree of kernel and the number of explanatory variables, and does not depend on the size of data set, M.

In order to apply our model to real data, we need to prepare several types of modified kernel model and need to investigate feasibility conditions for the induced LP problem.

REFERENCES

[1] M. A. Aizerman, E. M. Braverman, and L. I. Rozonoer, "Theoretical foundations of the potential function method in pattern recognition learning," *Automation and Remote Control*, Vol. 25, pp. 821837, 1964.

[2] A. Alim, F. T. Johora, S. Babu, and A. Sultana, "Elementary Operations on L-R Fuzzy Number," *Advanced in Pure Mathematics*, 5, pp. 131-136, 2015.

[3] M. Amagasa, "Formulation of A Sale Price Prediction Model Based on Fuzzy Regression Analysis," *Operations Research Proceedings 2011*, Springer Berlin Heidelberg, pp 567-572, 2012.

[4] M. Amagasa and K. Nagata, "Prediction Model with Interval Data - Toward Practical Applications-," *Proceedings of Information Processing and Management of Uncertainty in Knowledge-Based Systems(IPMU 2016)*, Part II, CCIS611, pp.213-224, 2016.

[5] N. Aronszajn, "Theory of reproducing kernels," *Transaction of the American Mathematical Society*, 68(3), pp.337-404, 1950.

[6] F. R. Bach and M. I. Jordan, "Kernel independent component analysis," *Journal of Machine Learning Research*, Vol. 3, pp.1-48, 2002.

[7] B. E. Boser, I. M. Guyon, V. N. Vapnik, "A training algorithm for optimal margin classifiers," *Proceedings of the fifth annual ACM workshop on Computational learning theory(COLT'92)*, pp. 144-152, ACM Press, 1992.

[8] P. D'Urso, "Linear regression analysis for fuzzy/crisp input and fuzzy/crisp output data," *Computational Statistics & Data Analysis*, 42, pp. 47-72, 2003.

[9] B. T. Gale, *Managing Customer Value*, FREE PRESS, 1994.

[10] P. Guo, and H. Tanaka, "Dual Models for Possibilistic Regression Analysis," *Computational Statistics & Data Analysis*, Vol.51(1), pp. 252-266, 2006.

[11] Y. Inoue, Y. Uematsu, M. Amagasa, and G. Tomizawa, "The method of setting forecast selling price model by fuzzy regression analysis," *Proceedings of Japan industrial Management Association*, Autumn Congress, pp.194-195, 1991.

[12] T. Melzer, M. Reiter, and H. Bischof, " Nonlinear feature extraction using generalized canonical correction analysis, " *Proceedings of Internal Conference Artificial Neural Networks(ICANN2001)*, pp.353-360, 2001.

[13] S. Mika, G. Rätsh, J. Weston, B. Schölkopf, and K.-R. Müller, "Fisher's discriminant analysis with kernels," *Neural Networks for Signal Processing,*, Vol. 11, pp. 41-48, IEEE, 1999.

[14] R. Rosipal and L. J. Trejo, "Kernel Partial Least Squares Regression in Reproducing Kernel Hilbert Space," *Journal of Machine Learning Research*, 2, pp. 97-123, 2001.

[15] B. Schölkopf, R. Herbrich, and A. J. Smola, " A Generalized Representer Theorem," *Proceedings of 14th Annual Conference on Computational Learning Theory and 5th European Conference on Computational Learning Theory*, pp. 416-426, Springer-Verlag, 2001.

[16] B. Schölkopf, A. J. Smola, and K.-R. Müller, " Nonlinear Component Analysis as a Kernel Eigenvalue Problem," *Neural Computation*, Vol. 10, No. 5, pp.1299-1319, MIT Press, 2006.

[17] J. Shawe-Taylor and N. Cristinanini, "Margin distribution and soft margin, " *Advanced in Large Margin Classifiers*, pp. 349-358, MIT Press, 2000.

[18] H. Tanaka, S. Uejima, and K. Asai, "Linear regression analysis with fuzzy model," IEEE Transactions on Systems, Man and Cybernetics, SMC-12, No.6, pp.903-907, 1982.

[19] H. Tanaka, "Fuzzy analysis by possibility linear models, " *Fuzzy Sets and Systems*, Vol.24, pp.363-375, 1987.

The Infiltration Game: Artificial Immune System for the Exploitation of Crime Relevant Information in Social Networks

Michael Spranger, Sven Becker, Florian Heinke, Hanna Siewerts and Dirk Labudde

University of Applied Sciences Mittweida
Forensic Science Investigation Lab (FoSIL), Germany
Email: spranger@hs-mittweida.de

Abstract—**Efficient and sensitive monitoring of social networks has become increasingly important for criminal investigations and crime prevention during the last years. However, with the growing amount of data and increasing complexity to be considered, monitoring tasks are difficult to handle, up to a point where manual observation is infeasible in most cases and, thus, automated systems are very much needed. In this paper, a system of adaptive agents is proposed, which aims at monitoring publicly accessible parts of a given social network for malign actions, such as propaganda, hate speeches or other malicious posts and comments made by groups or individuals. Subsequently, some of these agents try to gain access to crime relevant information exchanged in closed environments said individuals or groups are potentially part of. The presented monitoring and investigation processes are implemented by mimicking central aspects of the human immune system. The monitoring processes are realized by network-traversing informant units similar to pathogen-sensing macrophages, which initialize the human immune response. The subsequent investigation process is commenced by gathering information automatically about the targeted individual or group. Furthermore, based on the gathered information one can identify closed and usually inaccessible environments in the social network (e.g., private groups). Using so-called endoceptor units—automatically generated social bots imitating environment-typical appearance and communication—closed environments are accessed through individuals susceptible to the bot's strategy. Once being part of the closed network, an endoceptor aims to intercept and report back crime relevant communications and information to the investigators.**

Keywords–social network; prevention; predictive policing; text mining; autonomous agents; artificial immune system

I. Introduction

Over the last ten years, social networks have grown to become an essential part in our communication. Despite their success and advances made, social networks have also produced central hubs for criminal energy by providing the possibility/means to network as well as interchange and communicate ideas quickly, while remaining private in an environment difficult to control and monitor by investigators. Thus, for extreme political groups, criminal gangs and terrorist organizations, social networks are ideal platforms for planning and appointing the execution of criminal actions. Therefore, targeted monitoring of social networks can help to improve strategic security planning and prevention processes by authorities, as well as, help to increase the users' sense of security. Homeland security and secret services are aware of the importance of crucial information hidden in these networks and therefore more and more focus on social network surveillance. Looking at the increasing number of users worldwide – currently every third person uses social networks – there is a huge number of potential profiles and communication traffic to be monitored. This shows the need for an automated and sensitive solution that is able to cope with the vast amount of data and computational complexity yielding from it. Yet, besides these theoretical hurdles, the implementation of such monitoring procedures is further impaired due to the simple fact that in most cases crime-specific information is not discussed in the publicly accessible environment of social networks. Such relevant exchanges and discourses are rather made in closed inaccessible groups.

With respect to the legal limitations, in this work a multi-agent-based system is proposed, which aims at monitoring social networks and targeting potential offenders and (mostly) inaccessible subnetworks of their associates. The presented strategy utilizes a cascaded system of multi-role agent units, whose implementation and tasks are inspired by the human immune system. Similar to the cells involved in the human immune response (e.g., macrophages, killer cells and T-helper cells), the framework employs agents capable of sensing malicious actions, such as malign or offensive posts, analysing the profiles of the (potential) offenders, identifying the (mostly private and inaccessible) subnetworks of associates, entering these subnetworks as social bots that are automatically adapted to the appearances, ductus, and characteristic styles of these associates, and relaying explosive information exchanged in these subnetworks to the investigators.

In Section 2, we discuss related work presenting implementations of social network monitoring processes, as well as *in silico* realizations of the human response system and their applicability in this respect. Details about the proposed framework are presented in Section 3.

II. Related Work

Research conducted towards monitoring social media in the context of forensics has given rise to a large body of literature. In this section, a brief overview on works addressing this issue is given. Further, in order to put the proposed framework into context, some of the landmark papers discussing computational implementations of the human immune response system for data analyses are summarized. For a more in depth view, please refer to the notable review paper from Benkhelifa et al. [1] in which the authors outline some of the recent high-impact advancements and also propose a digital forensics incidents prediction framework tailored towards being utilized in cloud environments.

Complementing the idea of predicting future criminal incidents, in one of the most recent papers Soundarya et al. [2] elucidated the utilization of so-called genetic weighted k-means cluster analyses combined with negative selection schemes in an effort to make predictions based on social media profiling. Although the predictive power looks promising, implementing the presented prediction scheme successfully in real life applications is questionable, as underlying features used in their method are derived from information difficult to obtain in practice (e. g. the number of logins/sessions per day and the time duration of individual sessions). Another interesting idea was presented by Huber et al. [3]. Using their so-called Social Snapshot method, data can be efficiently acquired from social network websites that are of special interest for law enforcement agencies. This method is based on custom-made add-ons for crawling social networks and underlying web components. The Social Snapshots method further allows the extraction of profile information such as user data, private messages and images, and associated meta-data like internal timestamps and unique identifier. A prototype for Facebook was developed by the group and evaluated based on a volunteer survey.

Computational modelling of human immune response mechanisms and applying such models to various problems in data mining has been an ongoing research process for over two decades. In 2000, Timmis et al. [4] published an immune response-mimicking framework specifically designed for data analysis. Furthermore, the group presented a minimalistic formulation of an artificial immune system and elucidated its action/response mechanisms. As another example for application, Wu & Banzhaf [5] and West et al. [6] independently developed artificial immune systems for the detection of transactional frauds in automated bank machines. Both works employ binary matching rules paired with fuzzy logic in order to detect transaction anomalies. Chen et al. [7] discussed a classification technique, which considers some general aspects of immune response mechanisms. In combination with a population-based incremental adaptive learning scheme and collaborative filtering, their method aims at detecting invasive actions targeting computer networks. Finally, the research group of Karimi-Majd et al. [8] developed a novel hybrid artificial immune network for detecting sub-structures, so-called communities, in complex networks using statistical measures of structural network properties.

III. The Proposed Framework

The proposed multi-agent monitoring system, as illustrated in Figure 1, is inspired by the cellular mechanisms implemented by the human immune system. Although there are multiple immune response mechanisms and cell types with roles highly adapted to these individual mechanisms, the general concept of immune response can be summarized as follows: mobile recognition cells freely traversing the human body (e.g., macrophages) are able to recognize and absorb pathogens, such as viruses or infectious bacteria, and to report back pathogen-specific information upon which an adaptive immune response is triggered. Subsequently, mobile cells are synthesized that use the reported cellular information to specifically target and destroy invaded pathogens by means of a pathogen-specific molecular lock-and-key binding mechanism. Multiple aspects are implemented in the proposed framework that aim at mimicking this response concept in the context of recognizing hostile and malicious activities in the publicly accessible parts of the environment under investigation (e.g., selected profiles in (sub-) social networks, blogs or internet forums), and targeting groups of malign entities usually inaccessible to the public (e.g. closed groups in social networks).

The agent units implemented by the proposed framework are presented in more detail in the following subsections.

A. *Informants*

Similar to the biological role of pathogen-sensing macrophages, the task of informant units is to recognize potentially dangerous profiles within the social network. There are two basic types of informants, observers I^o and classifiers I^c. The objective of the observers is to read along public discussions, so called feeds. If a post or comment with potentially dangerous content is detected, the corresponding profile is reported as a candidate profile p^c to a central control unit, the agency Ψ (Implementation details about the agency are given later). The algorithmic layout of informants has to be manifold due to profile appearance variability of potential offenders. For example, to recognize the profile of a right-wing individual or organization, an analysis of the images on the profile or the members or friend lists can be helpful. In this respect, a binary classifier is trained for each feature, which is suitable to identify a particular type of potential offender. The training takes place in the form of semi-supervised learning. Candidate profiles whose membership to a certain potential offender type are considered to be secured serve as seeds. In order to minimize the likelihood of a misclassification, all classifiers of a certain type of potential offender form an ensemble which reports a profile as a candidate p^c to the agency by majority vote.

B. *Analysts*

The analysts A are specifically tailored towards certain groups of potential offenders. Their task is to gather information about candidate profiles. Such information could be, for example, the mood in the network determined by sentiment analyses, the development of its structural properties, or planned activities. As a special task, the analysts have to adapt to the language specificities of the respective group. In this way, on the one hand, the ability of the informants to discriminate profiles can be further improved. On the other hand, such specificities form the basis for the synthesis of adapted endoceptors. In the case of a group profile or the profile of an organization, the opinion-makers are detected by analysing the communication and subsequently reported to the agency. The detection of opinion-makers or multipliers can be conducted by considering the Page Rank algorithm [9] [10] or Hyperlink-Induced Topic Search (HITS) algorithm [11] developed to detect hubs and authorities on websites. Further informative features, such as hashtags, '@' references or information deduced from discourse analysis, need to be considered and are readily available in social network environments.

C. *Endoceptors*

The most subtle type of agents in the framework are endoceptors E. They are used when certain circumstances in the analysis justify the assumption that further explosive information is distributed in closed groups. Endoceptors are a kind of chat bot that adapts to the language behaviour of a potential offender group and tries to contact the leading members in order to become a member of the group. Once included, endoceptors remain passive and relay distributed information to the agency. In this way, they imitate the behaviour of a confidential informant.

D. Agency

In line with the human lymphatic system, a technical agency Ψ forms both the infrastructural basis of this framework and its bilateral interface to investigators. Such agencies include, in addition to the set of so-called candidate profiles P^c, a set of activation functions $\alpha_1, ..., \alpha_n$ as triggers for synthesizing different types of agents. A candidate profile in this respect can be the public profile of a group or organization but also the non-public one of an individual. A ranking $r(P^c)$ is assigned to each candidate, which determines whether and with which priority it is observed and which concrete actions, i. e., which concrete agent synthesis are triggered by the agency. Equation (1) shows that the ranking is mainly driven by two parts. The first part takes the frequency of notifications by observers into account. The second refers to the mean voting of all classifiers, whereat the individual influence can be adjusted by a weight w_i with $\sum w_i = 1$. For example, the classification of the profile of an organization as right-wing extremist might depend more on the estimation of the image classifier than the one who makes the same assessment by means of the list of friends. The influence of each part of the ranking function can be controlled by parameter λ with $\lambda = [0, 1]$, which needs to be estimated empirically.

$$r(p_i^c) = \lambda \frac{count(I^o, p_i^c)}{\sum_{P^c} count(I^o, p_j^c)} + (1 - \lambda) \sum_{j=1}^{|I^{c_j}|} \frac{w_j I^{c_j}(p_i^c)}{|I^{c_i}|} \quad (1)$$

The synthesis of an instance of a specific agent type is triggered by an activation function α. Equation (2) shows such a function for the activation of the analysts. The function decides on the basis of the rank of a candidate whether or not a threshold is exceeded and the synthesis is triggered. The threshold value can be regarded as a kind of intervention threshold. Thus, it represents a parameter for the implementation of safeguards against arbitrary surveillance.

$$\alpha_A(p_i^c) = \begin{cases} 1, & \text{if } r(p_i^c) > \epsilon \\ 0, & \text{otherwise} \end{cases} \quad (2)$$

E. Workflow

An illustration of the recognition and response mechanism is given in Figure 2. Individual monitoring steps are labelled A through E. The 'informant synthesis'—the *ad hoc* generation of informant units—is based on *a priori* expert knowledge provided by the investigators. The number of informants of a certain type of concept or topic to be monitored (illustrated by circle, square and triangle symbols) depends on the structural properties of the network and the amount of information exchanged by the users. Again, informants can only access publicly available information. Once public malicious activity is detected by an informant (see step A in Figure 2), entity-specific information is reported back to the agency (step B in Figure 2). In the illustration in A, an informant of type

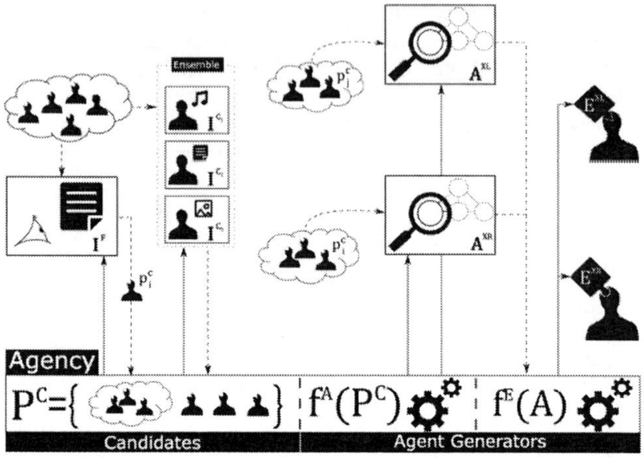

Figure 1. Schematic structure of the proposed framework. The informants I supply candidate profiles p^c to the agency where they are registered and evaluated by means of a ranking function. If a critical value is exceeded, analysts A are synthesized by a function f^A and sent out to collect information about these profiles. This information is the basis for endoceptors synthesized later by the function f^E attempt to infiltrate the protected areas of potentially dangerous profiles by contacting them in the manner of a chatbot by sending friendship requests. Once accepted, they remain passive and forward information to the investigating authorities.

'triangle' detects malicious activity in a subnetwork of users. Similarly, in B an informant of type 'cycle' reports an incident back to the agency. Subsequently, analyst unit synthesis is triggered according to an activation function (see Section III-D for formal details). The set of activation functions and their importance weighting relative to the number of detected incidents over time can be interpreted, in a biological sense, as the number of specific receptors for the different types of informants. The more 'alerted' informants are reporting back to the agency and are 'bound' to the agency, the more specific informants and receptors are subsequently synthesized. The ratio of synthesized receptors and informants bound to them illustrates the weight of the individual activation function. The role of the analyst unit is to use information retrieved from the publicly active malign entity to locate the network of associated malign entities and possible entry points to the subnetwork (step C in Figure 2). In a next step, this information is used to synthesize an endoceptor unit (step D in Figure 2). By mimicking the behaviour and appearance of target entities, the endoceptor aims at penetrating the closed environment, thus becoming a part of the network. Information exchanged by malign entities is now intercepted and communicated back to the agency module (step E in Figure 2).

IV. Conclusion and Future Work

In this work, we outlined a framework that allows investigators from law enforcement agencies and intelligence services to automatically monitor social networks and collect information about potentially dangerous activities. The framework is based on autonomous agents and inspired by the processes in the human immune system. However, no attention was paid to an exact replica of the biological processes. For the proposed framework, it is more important that the system is able to adapt itself to various disturbances. Therefore, it has to be able to adjust to the form of profiles of potential offenders, infiltrate

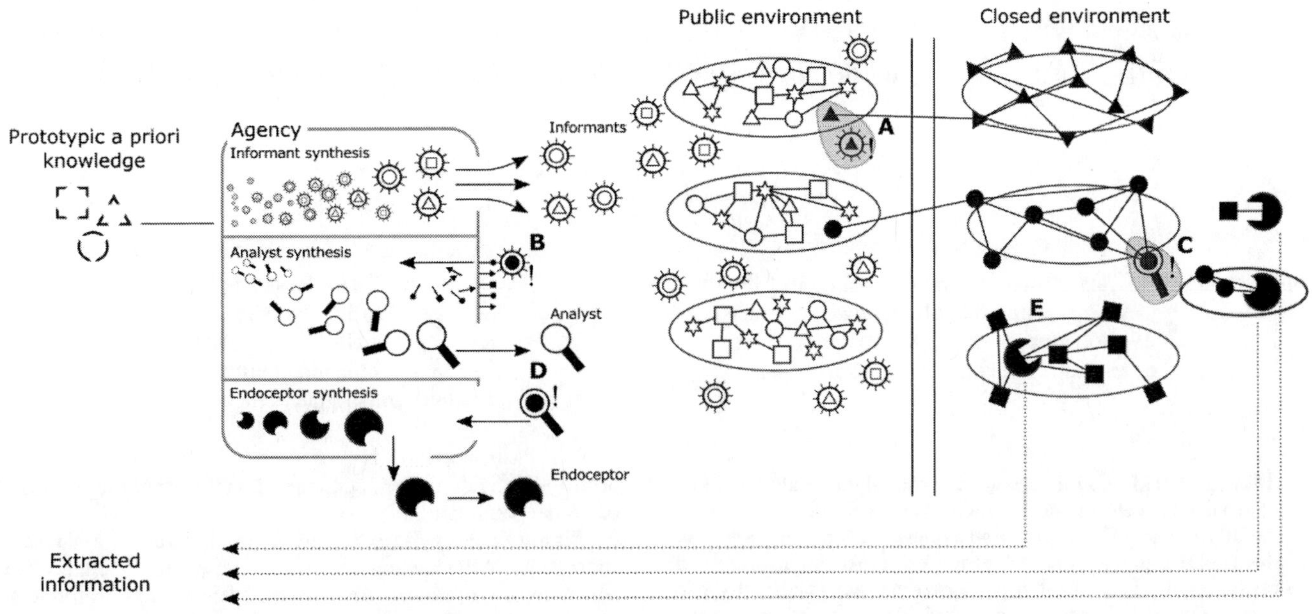

Figure 2. Schematic of the proposed workflow. Please refer to Section III-E for implementation details.

them and forward important information to the investigators. In this way, risks can be detected early and, at best, damage can be prevented.

Current and future work is mainly concerned with the design of the analysts, whereat the focus is on the detection of opinion-makers and the analysis of language style and writing behaviour in the group as a prerequisite for the synthesis of chat bots (Endoceptors) that are recognized by that group as their peers. As a by-product, we can learn how chat bots can be detected in networks. In parallel, independent sets of social features have to be found, which are suitable to classify candidates with the necessary accuracy to address privacy concerns.

REFERENCES

[1] E. Benkhelifa, E. Rowe, R. Kinmond, O. A. Adedugbe, and T. Welsh, "Exploiting social networks for the prediction of social and civil unrest: A cloud based framework," in Future Internet of Things and Cloud (FiCloud), 2014 International Conference on. IEEE, 2014, pp. 565–572.

[2] V. Soundarya, U. Kanimozhi, and D. Manjula, "Recommendation system for criminal behavioral analysis on social network using genetic weighted k-means clustering." JCP, vol. 12, no. 3, 2017, pp. 212–220.

[3] M. Huber, M. Mulazzani, M. Leithner, S. Schrittwieser, G. Wondracek, and E. Weippl, "Social snapshots: Digital forensics for online social networks," in Proceedings of the 27th annual computer security applications conference. ACM, 2011, pp. 113–122.

[4] J. Timmis, M. Neal, and J. Hunt, "An artificial immune system for data analysis," Biosystems, vol. 55, no. 1, 2000, pp. 143–150.

[5] S. X. Wu and W. Banzhaf, "Combatting financial fraud: a coevolutionary anomaly detection approach," in Proceedings of the 10th annual conference on Genetic and evolutionary computation. ACM, 2008, pp. 1673–1680.

[6] J. West, M. Bhattacharya, and R. Islam, "Intelligent financial fraud detection practices: An investigation," in International Conference on Security and Privacy in Communication Systems. Springer, 2014, pp. 186–203.

[7] M.-H. Chen, P.-C. Chang, and J.-L. Wu, "A population-based incremental learning approach with artificial immune system for network intrusion detection," Engineering Applications of Artificial Intelligence, vol. 51, 2016, pp. 171–181.

[8] A.-M. Karimi-Majd, M. Fathian, and B. Amiri, "A hybrid artificial immune network for detecting communities in complex networks," Computing, vol. 97, no. 5, 2015, pp. 483–507.

[9] S. Brin and L. Page, "The anatomy of a large-scale hypertextual web search engine," Comput. Netw. ISDN Syst., vol. 30, no. 1-7, Apr. 1998, pp. 107–117. [Online]. Available: http://dx.doi.org/10.1016/S0169-7552(98)00110-X

[10] ——, "The anatomy of a large-scale hypertextual web search engine," in Proceedings of the Seventh International Conference on World Wide Web 7, ser. WWW7. Amsterdam, The Netherlands, The Netherlands: Elsevier Science Publishers B. V., 1998, pp. 107–117. [Online]. Available: http://dl.acm.org/citation.cfm?id=297805.297827

[11] J. M. Kleinberg, "Authoritative sources in a hyperlinked environment," J. ACM, vol. 46, no. 5, Sep. 1999, pp. 604–632. [Online]. Available: http://doi.acm.org/10.1145/324133.324140

[12] M. Spranger, S. Schildbach, F. Heinke, S. Grunert, and D. Labudde, "Semantic tools for forensics: A highly adaptable framework," in Proc. 2nd. International Conference on Advances in Information Management and Mining (IMMM), IARIA. ThinkMind Library, 2012, pp. 27–31.

[13] C. Weinstein, W. Campbell, B. Delaney, and G. O'Leary, "Modeling and detection techniques for counter-terror social network analysis and intent recognition," in 2009 IEEE Aerospace conference, 2009, pp. 1–16.

Understanding the Food Supply Chain using Social Media Data Analysis

Nagesh Shukla
SMART Infrastructure Facility, Faculty of EIS
University of Wollongong
Wollongong, NSW 2500, Australia
e-mail: nshukla@uow.edu.au

Nishikant Mishra, Akshit Singh
Hull University Business School
Hull University
Hull HU6 7RX, UK
e-mail: n.mishra@hull.ac.uk
e-mail: akshit.singh@manchester.ac.uk

***Abstract*— This paper proposes a big data analytics based approach, which considers social media (Twitter) data for identifying supply chain management issues in food industries. In particular, the proposed approach includes: (i) capturing of relevant tweets based on keywords; (ii) pre-processing of the raw tweets; and, (iii) text analysis using support vector machine (SVM) and hierarchical clustering with multiscale bootstrap resampling. The result of this approach included cluster of words, which can inform supply chain (SC) decision makers about the customer feedback and issues in the flow/quality of the food products. A case study of the beef supply chain was analysed using the proposed approach where three weeks of data from Twitter was used. The results indicated that the proposed text analytic approach can be helpful to efficiently identify and summarise crucial customer feedback for supply chain management.**

Keywords- Twitter data; social media; data mining; clustering.

I. INTRODUCTION

With the advent of online social media, there is lot of consumer information available on Twitter, which reflects the true opinion of customers [9]. Effective analysis of this information can give interesting insight into consumer sentiments and behaviors with respect to one or more specific issues. Using social media data, a retailer can capture a real-time overview of consumer reactions about an episodic event. Social media data is relatively cheap and can be very effective in gathering opinion of large and diverse audiences. Using different information techniques, business organisations can collect social media data in real time and can use it for developing future strategies. However, social media data is qualitative and unstructured in nature and often large in volume, variety and velocity [6]. At times, it is difficult to handle it using traditional operation and management tools and techniques for business purposes. In the past, social media analytics have been implemented in various supply chain problems predominantly in manufacturing supply chains. The research on application of social media analytics in domain of food supply chain is in its primitive stage. In this article, an attempt has been made to use social media data in domain of food supply chain to make it consumer centric. The results from the analysis have been linked with all the segments of supply chain to improve customer satisfaction.

Firstly, data was extracted from Twitter (via Twitter streaming API) using relevant keywords related to consumer's opinion about different food products. Thereafter, pre-processing and text mining was performed to investigate the positive and negative sentiments of tweets using Support Vector Machine (SVM). Hierarchical clustering of tweets from different geographical locations (World, UK, Australia and USA) using multiscale bootstrap resampling was performed. Further, root causes of issues affecting consumer satisfaction were identified and linked with various segments of supply chain to make it more efficient. Finally, the recommendations for consumer centric supply chain were described.

This paper is organized as follows. Section II, presents the literature review related to food products supply chain and state-of-the-art methods used in the area. In Section III, the proposed methodology is discussed in detail. Section IV presents the results obtained by applying proposed twitter based analytics for beef supply chain. Section V details the managerial implications of the proposed analysis method in food products supply chain. Finally, Section VI concludes this research with some guidelines for future research.

II. LITERATURE REVIEW

Food products supply chain, such as for beef products consists of various stakeholders, which are farmer, abattoir and processor, retailer and consumer. Literature consists of research publications on diverse characteristics of beef supply chain such as waste minimisation, vertical coordination in supply chain, traceability, greenhouse gas emission, meat quality, meat safety. For instance, Francis et al. [4] have applied value chain analysis for examination of beef sector in UK. The opportunities for waste minimisation at producer and processor level have been identified in the UK by comparing them to practices followed in Argentina. Consequently, good management practices have been suggested to mitigate the waste generated in UK beef industry. Wang et al. [16] have utilised the standardized performance analysis data to examine the beef farms in Texas Rolling plants.

In literature, several types of framework have been proposed to investigate problems and issues associated with supply chain through big data analysis. Chae [1] has developed a Twitter analytics framework for evaluation of Twitter information in the field of supply chain management. An attempt has been made by them to fathom the potential engagement of Twitter in the application of supply chain management and further research and development. Tan et al. [14] have suggested an analytic mechanism for capturing and processing of big data generated in the corporate world. It employed deduction graph technique. Hazen et al. [7] have determined the problems associated with quality of data in the field of supply chain management and a novel procedure for monitoring and managing of data quality was suggested. Vera-Baquero et al. [15] have recommended a cloud-based mechanism utilising big data procedures to efficiently improve the performance analysis of corporations. Frizzo et al. [5] have done a thorough analysis of literature on big data available in reputed business journals. A very limited work is being done to explore the characteristics of food supply chain by utilising social media data.

Twitter, Facebook and Youtube denote the swift expansion of Web2.0 and applications on social media lately. Twitter is the most rapidly growing social media platform since its outset in 2006. More than 75% of corporate firms enlisted in Fortune Global 100 have one or more Twitter account for the entire firm and for their distinct brands [10]. This research study will use Twitter data for the identifying issues in supply chain management (SCM) in food industries. The next section describes the research study conducted in this paper.

III. Analytics Approach

In case of social media data analysis, three major issues are to be considered, namely, data harvesting/capturing, data storage, and data analysis. Data capturing in case of twitter starts with finding the topic of interest by using appropriate keywords list (including texts and hashtags). This keywords list is used together with the twitter streaming APIs to gather publicly available datasets from the twitter postings. Twitter streaming APIs allows data analysts to collect 1% of available Twitter datasets. There are other third party commercial data providers like Firehose with full historical twitter datasets.

The Twitter streaming API allowed us to store/append twitter data in a text file. The analysis of the gathered Twitter data is generally complex due to the presence of unstructured textual information, which typically requires Natural Language Processing (NLP) algorithms. We proposed two main types of content analysis techniques – sentiment mining and clustering analysis for investigating the extracted Twitter data; see Figure 1. More information about the proposed sentiment mining method and hierarchical clustering method is detailed in the following subsections.

A. Data Analysis

The information available on social media is predominantly in the unstructured textual format. Therefore, it is essential to employ Content Analysis (CA) approaches, which includes a wide array of text mining and NLP methods to accumulate knowledge from Web 2.0 [2]. An appropriate cleaning of text and further processing is required for effective knowledge gathering. There is no best way to perform data cleaning and several applications have used their own heuristics to clean the data. A text cleaning exercise, which included removal of extra spaces, punctuation, numbers, symbols, and html links were used. Then, a list of major food retailers in the world (including their names and Twitter handles) was used to filter and select a subset of tweets, which are used for analysis.

1) Sentiment analysis based on SVM

Tweets contain sentiments as well as information about the topic. Thus, sophisticated text mining procedures like sentiment analysis are vital for extracting true customer opinion. The objective here is to categorise each tweet with positive and negative sentiment. Sentiment analysis, which is also widely known as opinion mining is defined as the domain of research that evaluates public's sentiments, appraisals, attitudes, emotions, evaluations, opinions towards various commodities like services, corporations, products, problems, situations, subjects and their characteristics.

The identification of polarity mentioned in opinion is a crucial for transforming the format of opinion from text to numeric value. The performance of data mining methods such as SVM is excellent for sentiment classification. SVM model is employed in this approach for the division of polarity of opinions. Initially, a set of features from the data must be chosen. In this case, we have used Unigrams and Bigrams, which are the tokens of one-word and two-word, respectively, identified from the tweets. In this study, we used binary value {0,1} to represent the presence of these features in the microblog.

SVM is a technique for supervised machine learning, which requires a training data set to identify best Maximum Margin Hyperplane (MMH). In the past, researchers have used approach where they have manually analysed and marked data prior to their use as training data set. In this case, we have examined the use of emoticons to identify sentiment of opinions. In this paper, Twitter data was pre-processed based on emoticons to create training dataset for SVM. Microblogs with ":)" were marked as "+1" representing positive polarity, whereas messages with ":(" were marked as "-1" representing negative polarity. It was observed that more than 89% messages were marked precisely by following this procedure. Thus, the training data set was captured using this approach for SVM analysis. Then, a grid search (Hsu et al., 2003) was employed to train SVM. The polarity (Pol_m={+1,-1}) representing positive and negative sentiment respectively of microblog m can be predicted using trained SVM. In real life, when consumers buy beef products, they leave their true opinion (feedback) on Twitter. In this article, the SVM classifier has been utilised to classify these sentiments into positive and negative and consequently gather intelligence from these tweets.

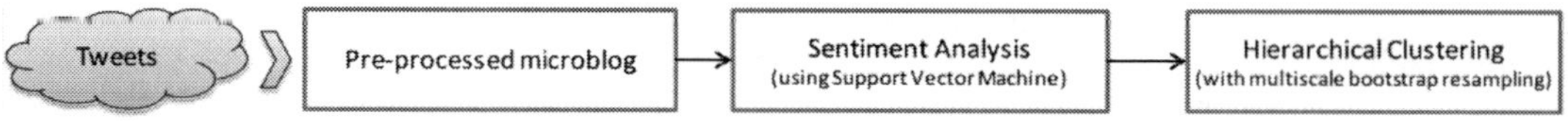

Figure 1. Overall approach for social media data analysis

2) Hierarchical clustering with p-values using multiscale bootstrap resampling

In this research, we also employed a hierarchical clustering with p-values via multiscale bootstrap resampling method to analyse the content of tweets with positive and negative sentiments [13]. The clustering method creates hierarchical clusters of words and also computes their significance using p-values (obtained after multiscale bootstrap resampling). This helps in easily identifying significant clusters in the datasets and their hierarchy. The agglomerative method used is ward.D2 [11]

In a typical data clustering approach, data support for the identified clusters is not present. The support of data for these clusters can be obtained by adopting multiscale bootstrap resampling. In this approach, the dataset is replicated by resampling for large number of times and the hierarchical clustering is applied. During resampling, replicating sample sizes was changed to multiple values including smaller, larger and equal to the original sample size. Then, bootstrap probabilities are determined by counting the number of dendrograms, which contained a particular cluster and dividing it by the number of bootstrap samples. This is done for all the clusters and sample sizes. Then, these bootstrap probabilities are used to estimate p-value, which is also known as Approximately Unbiased (AU) value.

The result of hierarchical clustering with multiscale bootstrap resampling is a cluster dendrogram. At every stage, the two clusters, which have the highest resemblance are combined to form one new cluster. The distance or dissimilarity between the clusters is denoted by the vertical axis of dendrogram. The various items and clusters are represented on horizontal axis. It also illustrates several values at branches, such as AU p-values (left), Bootstrap Probability (BP) values (right), and cluster labels (bottom). Clusters with AU >= 95% are usually shown by the red rectangles, which represents significant clusters.

IV. Results and Discussion

The proposed Twitter data analysis approach is used to understand issues related to the beef/steak supply chain based on consumer feedback on Twitter. This analysis can help to analyse reasons for positive and negative sentiments, identify communication patterns, prevalent topics and content, and characteristics of Twitter users discussing about beef and steak. Based on the result of the proposed analysis, a set of recommendations have been prescribed for developing customer centric supply chain. The total number of tweets extracted for this research was 1,338,638 (as per the procedure discussed in Section 3). They were captured from 23/03/2016 to 13/04/2016 using the keywords beef and steak. Only tweets in English language were considered with no geographic constraint. Figure 2 shows the geo-located tweets in the collected dataset. Then, keywords were selected to capture the tweets relevant to this study. The overall tweets were then filtered using this list of keywords so that only the relevant tweets (26,269) are retrieved. Then, country wise classification of tweets was performed by using the name of supermarket corresponding to each country. It was observed that tweets from USA, UK and Australia and World were 1605, 822, 338 and 15214 respectively. There were many hashtags observed in the collected tweets. The most frequently used hashtags (more than 1000) were highlighted in Table 1.

As described in the previous subsection, the collection of training data for SVM was done automatically based on emoticons. The training data was developed by collecting 10,664 messages from the Twitter data captured with emoticons ":)" and ":(". The automatic marking process concluded by generating 8560 positive, 2104 negative and 143 discarded messages. Positive and negative messages were then randomly classified into five categories. The 8531 messages in first four categories were utilised as training data set and the rest of the 2133 messages were utilised as the test data set.

Numerous pre-processing steps were employed to minimise the number of features prior to implementing SVM training. Initially, the target query and terms related to topic (beef/steak related words) were deleted to prevent the classifier from categorising sentiment based on certain queries or topics. Various feature sets were collected and their accuracy level was examined. In terms of performance of the classifier, we have used two types of indicators: (i) 5-fold cross validation (CV) accuracy, and (ii) the accuracy level obtained when trained SVM is used to predict sentiment of test data set.

Table 2 reports the performance of SVM based classifiers on the collected microblogs. The best performance is provided when using unigram feature set in both SVM and Naïve Bayes classifiers. The unigram feature set gives better result than the other feature sets. This is due to the fact that additional casual and new terms are utilised to express the emotions. It negatively affects the precision of subjective word set characteristic as it is based on a dictionary. Also, the binary representation scheme produced comparable results, except for unigrams, with those produced by term frequency (TF) based representation schemes. As the length of micro blogging posts are quite short, binary representation scheme and TF representation scheme are similar and have almost matching performance levels. Therefore, the SVM based classifier with unigrams as feature set represented in binary scheme is used for estimating the sentiment score of the microblog.

Figure 2. Visualisation of tweets with geolocation data

TABLE 1. TOP HASHTAGS USED

Hashtag	Freq (>1000)	Freq (%)	Hashtag	Freq (>1000)	Freq (%)
#beef	17708	16.24%	#aodafail	1908	1.75%
#steak	14496	13.29%	#earls	1859	1.70%
#food	7418	6.80%	#votemainefpp	1795	1.65%
#foodporn	5028	4.61%	#win	1761	1.62%
#whcd	5001	4.59%	#ad	1754	1.61%
#foodie	4219	3.87%	#cooking	1688	1.55%
#recipe	4106	3.77%	#mplusplaces	1686	1.55%
#boycottearls	3356	3.08%	#meat	1607	1.47%
#gbbw	3354	3.08%	#lunch	1577	1.45%
#kca	2898	2.66%	#bbq	1557	1.43%
#dinner	2724	2.50%	#yum	1424	1.31%
#recipes	2159	1.98%	#yummy	1257	1.15%
#accessibility	1999	1.83%	#bdg	1255	1.15%

TABLE 2. PERFORMANCE OF SVM BASED CLASSIFIER ON SELECTED FEATURE SETS

Representation scheme	Feature Type	Number of Features	SVM	
			CV (%)	Test data (%)
Binary	Unigram	12,257	91.75	90.80
	Bigram	44,485	76.80	74.46
	Unigram + bigram	56,438	87.12	83.28
Term Frequency	Unigram	12,257	88.78	86.27
	Bigram	44,485	77.49	71.68
	Unigram + bigram	56,438	84.81	80.97

To identify meaningful content in the collected tweets, initially, we performed sentiment analysis to identify sentiments of each of the tweets followed by HCA. Following section provides the results of the analysis performed on the tweets (by sentiment) collected worldwide and UK.

a) Analysis of negative tweets from the world

The collected tweets were divided into positive and negative sentiment tweets. In negative sentiment tweets, the most frequently used words associated with 'beef' and 'steak', were 'smell', 'recipe', 'deal', 'colour', 'spicy', 'taste' and 'bone.' Cluster analysis is performed on the negative tweets from the world to divide them into clusters in terms of resemblance among their tweets. The three predominant clusters identified (with significance >0.95 level) are represented in Figure 3 as red coloured rectangles. The first cluster consists of bone and broth, which highlights the excess of bone fragments in broth. The second cluster is composed of jerky and smell. The customers have expressed their annoyance with the bad smell associated with jerky. The third cluster consists of tweets comprising of taste and deal. Customers have often complained to the supermarket about the bad flavour of the beef products bought within the promotion (deal). The rest of the words highlighted in Figure 3 does not lead to any conclusive remarks.

This cluster analysis will help global supermarkets to identify the major issues faced by customers. It will provide them the opportunity to mitigate these problems and raise customer satisfaction and their consequent revenue.

TABLE 3. RAW TWEETS WITH SENTIMENT POLARITY

Sentiment	Raw Tweets
Negative	*@Morrisons so you have no comment about the lack of meat in your Family Steak Pie? #morrisons*
Negative	*@AsdaServiceTeam why does my rump steak from asda Kingswood taste distinctly of bleach please?*
Positive	*Wonderful @marksandspencer are now selling #glutenfree steak pies and they are delicious and perfect! Superb stuff.*
Positive	*Ive got one of your tesco finest* beef Chianti's in the microwave oven right now and im pretty pleased about it if im honest*

b) Analysis of negative tweets from UK

The most widely used words after 'beef' and 'steak' were 'tesco', 'coffee', 'asda', 'aldi'. The association rule mining indicated that the word 'beef' was most closely associated with terms like 'brisket', 'rosemary', and 'cooker', etc. It was least used with terms like 'tesco', 'stock', 'bit'. The word 'steak' was highly associated with 'absolute', 'back', 'flat'. and rarely associated with words like 'stealing', 'locked', 'drug'.

The four predominant clusters are identified (with significance >0.95 level). The first cluster contains the words – man, coffee, dunfermline, stealing, locked, addict, drug. When this cluster was analysed together with raw tweets, it was found that this cluster represents an event where a man was caught stealing coffee and steak from a major food store in 'Dunfermline'. The finding from this cluster is not linked to our study. However, it could assist retailers for various purposes such as developing strategy for an efficient security system in stores to address shoplifting. Cluster 2 is related to the tweets discussing high prices of steak meal deals. Cluster 3 represents the concerns of users on the use of horsemeat in many beef products offered by major superstores. It reveals that consumer are concerned about the traceability of beef products. Cluster 4 groups tweets, which discuss the lack of locally produced British sliced beef in the major stores (with #BackBritishFarming). It reflects that consumers prefer the beef derived from British cattle instead of imported beef. Rest of the clusters, when analysed together with raw tweets, did not highlight any conclusive remarks and users were discussing mainly one-off problems with cooking and cutting slices of beef.

The proposed HCA can help to identify (in an automated manner) root causes of the issues with the currently sold beef and steak products. This can help major superstores to monitor and respond quickly to the customer issues raised in the social media platforms.

V. MANAGERIAL IMPLICATIONS

The finding of this study can assist the beef retailers to develop a consumer centric supply chain. During the analysis, it was found that sometimes, consumers were unhappy because of high price of steak products, lack of local meat, bad smell, presence of bone fragments, lack of tenderness, cooking time and overall quality. In a study, Wrap (2008) estimated that 161,000 tones of meat waste occurred because of customer dissatisfaction. The majority of food waste is because of discoloration, bad flavor, smell, packaging issues, and presence of foreign body. Discoloration can be solved by using new packaging technologies and by utilising natural antioxidants in the diet of cattle. If the cattle consumes fresh grass before slaughtering, it can help to increase the Vitamin E in the meat and have a huge impact on delaying the oxidation of color and lipid. The issues related to bad smell and flavor can be caused due to temperature abuse of beef products. The efficient cold chain management throughout the supply chain, raising awareness and proper coordination among different stakeholders can assist retailers to overcome this issue. The packaging of beef products can be affected by mishandling during the product flow in the supply chain or by following inefficient packaging techniques by abattoir and processor, which can also lead to presence of foreign body within beef products. Inefficient packaging affects the quality, color, taste and smell. Periodic maintenance of packaging machines and using more advanced packaging techniques like modified atmosphere packaging and vacuum skin packaging will assist retailers in addressing above mentioned issues.

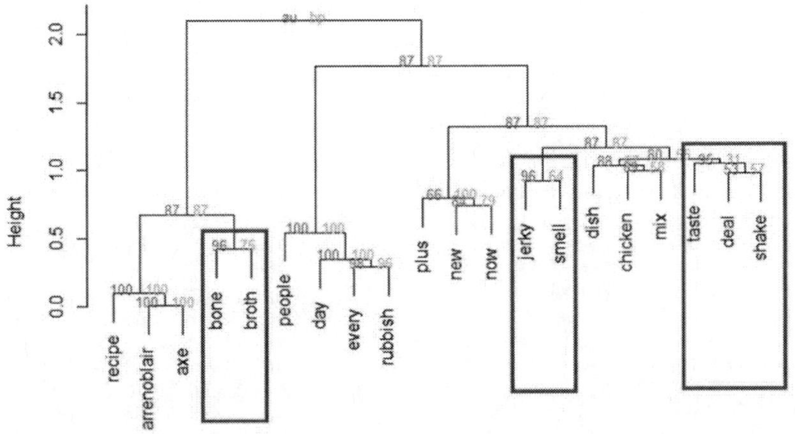

Figure 3. Hierarchical cluster analysis of the negative tweets originating in the World

The high price of beef products can be mitigated by improving the vertical coordination within the beef supply chain. The lack of coordination in the supply chain leads to waste, which results in high price of beef products. Therefore, a strategic planning and its implementation can assist the food retailers to reduce price of their beef products more efficiently than their rivals.

During the analysis, it was found that products made from forequarter and hindquarter of cattle have different patterns of demand in the market, which leads to carcass imbalance [3][12]. It leads to huge loss to retailers and contribute to food waste. Sometimes, consumers think that meat derived from different cuts such as forequarter and hindquarter have different attributes like flavor, tenderness, and cooking time as well as price. The hindquarter products like steak and joint are tenderer, takes less time for cooking and are more expensive whereas forequarter products like mince and burger have less tenderness, takes more time for cooking and are relatively cheaper. Consumers think that beef products derived from the forequarter and hindquarter have different taste and it affects their buying behavior. In this study, it was found that slow cooking methods like casseroling, stewing, pot- roasting and braising can improve the flavor and tenderness of forequarter products. With the help of proper marketing, advertisement, retailers can raise awareness between the consumers and can increase the demand of less favorable beef products, which will further assist in waste minimization and making the supply chain more customer centric.

The analysis of consumer tweets reveal that consumers especially from the UK, were interested in consuming local beef products. Their main concern was quality and food safety. Specially, after horsemeat scandal, customers are prone towards traceability information, i.e., information related to animal breed, slaughtering method, animal welfare, use of pesticides, hormones and other veterinary drugs in beef farms. Retailers can gain the consumer confidence by following the strict traceability regime within the supply chain.

VI. Conclusions and Future Work

Consumers have started to express their views on social media. Using social media data, a company can know the perception of their existing or potential consumers about them and their business rivals. In this study, Twitter data has been used to investigate the consumer sentiments. More than one million tweets related to beef products has been collected using different keywords. Text mining has been performed to investigate positive and negative sentiments of the consumers. During the analysis, it was found that the main concern related to beef products among consumers were color, food safety, smell, flavor and presence of foreign body in beef products. These issues generate huge disappointment among consumers. There were a lot of tweets related to positive sentiments where consumers had discovered and share their experience about promotion, deal and a particular combination of food and drinks with beef products. Based on the findings, some recommendations has been prescribed to develop consumer centric supply chain. In future, extensive list of keywords can be used for further analysis. Future work may include standardizing the data preprocessing steps for better model training and prediction. For instance, positive and negative words can be included in the analysis for better sentiment prediction. Network analysis tools can be also employed to understand the social network communities and identifying marketing opportunities.

References

[1] B. K. Chae, "Insights from hashtag# supplychain and Twitter analytics: Considering Twitter and Twitter data for supply chain practice and research," International Journal of Production Economics, vol. 165, pp. 247-259, 2015.

[2] M. Chau and J. Xu, "Business intelligence in blogs: Understanding consumer interactions and communities," MIS quarterly, vol. 36, no. 4, pp. 1189-1216, 2012.

[3] A. Cox and D. Chicksand, "The Limits of Lean Management Thinking: Multiple Retailers and Food and Farming Supply Chains," European Management Journal, vol. 23, no. 6, pp. 648-662, 2005.

[4] M. Francis, D. Simons and M. Bourlakis, "Value chain analysis in the UK beef foodservice sector," Supply chain management: an international journal, vol. 13, no. 1, pp. 83-91, 2008.

[5] J. Frizzo- Barker, P. A. Chow-White, M. Mozafari, D. Ha, "An empirical study of the rise of big data in business scholarship," International Journal of Information Management, vol. 36, pp. 403-413, 2016.

[6] I. A. T. Hashem, I. Yaqoob, N. B. Anuar, S. Mokhtar, A. Gani, S. U. Khan, "The rise of "big data" on cloud computing: Review and open research issues," Information Systems, vol. 47, pp. 98-115, 2015.

[7] B. T. Hazen, C. A. Boone, J. D. Ezell, L. A. Jones-Farmer, "Data quality for data science, predictive analytics, and big data in supply chain management: An introduction to the problem and suggestions for research and applications," International Journal of Prod. Economics, vol. 154, pp. 72-80, 2016.

[8] C. W. Hsu, C. C. Chang and C. J. Lin, "A Practical Guide to Support Vector Classification," Technical report, Department of Computer Science and Information Engineering, National Taiwan University, Taipei, 2003.

[9] P. W. Liang and B. R. Dai, "Opinion mining on social media data" In 2013 IEEE 14th International Conference on Mobile Data Management, vol. 2, pp. 91-96, 2013.

[10] A. C. Malhotra, C. K. Malhotra and A. See, "How to get your messages retweeted" MIT Sloan Management Review, vol. 53, no. 2, pp. 61-76, 2012.

[11] F. Murtagh and P. Legendre, "Ward's hierarchical agglomerative clustering method: which algorithms implement Ward's criterion?", Journal of Classification, vol. 31, no. 3, pp. 274-295, 2014.

[12] D. Simons, M. Francis, M. Bourlakis, A. Fearne, "Identifying the determinants of value in the UK red meat industry: A value chain analysis approach," Journal on Chain and Network Science, vol. 3, no. 2, pp. 109-121, 2003.

[13] R. Suzuki and H. Shimodaira, "Pvclust: an R package for assessing the uncertainty in hierarchical clustering", Bioinformatics, vol. 22, no. 12, pp. 1540-1542, 2006.

[14] K. H. Tan, Y. Zhan, G. Ji, F. Ye, C. Chang, "Harvesting big data to enhance supply chain innovation capabilities: An analytic infrastructure based on deduction graph," International Journal of Production Economics, vol. 165, pp. 223-233, 2015.

[15] A. Vera-Baquero, R. Colomo-Palacios and O. Molloy, "Real-time business activity monitoring and analysis of process performance on big-data domains," Telematics and Informatics, vol. 33, no. 3, pp. 793-807, 2016.

[16] T. Wang, S. C. Park, S. Bevers, R. Teague, J. Cho, "Factors affecting cow-calf herd performance and greenhouse gas emissions," Journal of Agricultural and Resource Economics, vol. 38, no. 3, pp. 435-456, 2013.

[17] Warp Report. The food we waste, http://www.ifr.ac.uk/waste/ Reports/ WRAP%20The%20Food%20We%20Waste.pdf, Accessed: 28/04/2017, ISBN:1844053830, 2008.

A Framework for Blog Data collection: Challenges and Opportunities

Muhammad Nihal Hussain, Adewale Obadimu, Kiran Kumar Bandeli, Mohammad Nooman, Samer Al-khateeb, Nitin Agarwal[†]
[†]Jerry L. Maulden-Entergy Chair Professor of Information Science
University of Arkansas at Little Rock, Little Rock, United States
e-mails: {mnhussain, amobadimu, kxbandeli, msnooman, sxalkhateeb, nxagarwal}@ualr.edu

Abstract—**Blogosphere has, although slowly after the advent of Twitter, continued to rise and provides a rich medium for content framing. With no restriction on the number of characters, many users use blogs to express their opinion and use other social media channels like Twitter and Facebook to steer their audience to their blogs. Blogs provide more content than any other social media and serve as a good platform for agenda-setting. This content can be of great use to sociologists and data scientists to track opinions about events. However, the importance of blog tracking has been challenged due to the complex process of data collection and handling unstructured text data. This has caused many tracking tools to abandon blogs and move to other medium like Twitter. Nevertheless, blogs continue to be an important part of social media and cannot be ignored. In this paper, we explain the process to collect blog data, challenges we encounter, and demonstrate the importance of blog tracking through a real-world test case. The blog datasets discussed in this paper are made available publicly for researchers and practitioners through the Blogtrackers tool.**

Keywords-blog; unstructured data; web crawling; blog data collection; blog data analysis tool.

I. INTRODUCTION

The advent of participatory Web applications (or Web 2.0 [1]) have created online media that has turned the former mass information consumer to the present information producer [2]. Examples include blogs, wikis, social annotation and tagging, media sharing, and various other services. A blog site or simply blog (short for web log) is a collection of entries by individuals displayed in reverse chronological order. These entries, known as blog posts, can typically combine text, images, and URLs (Uniform Resource Locator) pointing to other blogs and/or to other Web pages. Blogging is becoming a popular means for mass Web users to express, communicate, share, collaborate, debate, and reflect. WordPress, a popular blogging platform, reports that more than 80.7 million blog posts are generated each month [3].

Blogosphere is a virtual universe that contains all blogs. Blogosphere also represents a network of blogs where each node could be either a blog or a blog post and the edges depict a hyperlink between two nodes in the Blogosphere. Bloggers, the blog post writers/authors, loosely form their special interest communities; where they share thoughts, express opinions, debate ideas, and offer suggestions interactively. Blogosphere provides a conducive platform to build virtual communities of special interests. It reshapes business models [4], assists viral marketing [5], provides trend analysis and sales prediction [6][7], aids counter-terrorism effort [8], and acts as grassroots information sources [9].

A typical blog has different posts written by one author or multiple authors on various topics of interests or activities/events occurring around the world. Blogs and other similar participatory media afford democratic spaces for people to discuss and share views that may not be endorsed by mainstream media or even traditional journalism. Additionally, the commentaries or discussions are kept for others to view and contribute further. All these features make blogs a great platform for supporting citizen journalism initiatives. Such initiatives are essential for the democratic processes of production, dissemination, and reception of news. However, one need not look farther than the current political climate to comprehend the dangers of the freedom of the Internet. Blogging and other participatory media have been strategically used to disseminate falsehoods, rumors, and gossips, to provoke hysteria, or even delegitimize governments [10][11]. Therefore, it is important to understand the blogosphere; to explore information consumption behavior of individuals, and moreover, to shed insights on how misinformation originates and spreads.

Analyzing blogs data help in understanding the pulse of a society, knowing what resonates with a community, and recognizing grievances of a group, among other reasons. Since blogs have no limit on the space available for expressing and/or discussing a topic of interest, blogs improve quality and inclusiveness of discourse and serve as a place for developing narratives. Blogs also provide a convenient platform to develop situational awareness during a socio-political crisis or humanitarian crisis in a conflict-torn region or a natural disaster struck area. While 'big' social data, especially blogs, offer promise for analysis and situational understanding [12], it also imposes significant challenges. Some of the challenges impacting this area of research are: architectural and collection issues, keeping the data up to date, processing requirements, data storage, privacy considerations, incongruities of data forms and scales, trustworthiness and reliability of the source material, and vastly varied availability of data, etc. This paper addresses key challenges pertaining to architectural and data collection issues, data cleaning, data processing, and analyzing and extracting actionable insights from blog datasets. The blog datasets discussed in this paper are made publicly available for researchers and practitioners through the Blogtrackers tool [13].

The rest of this paper is organized as follows. Section II describes the current state of blog data collection. Section III describes the methodology for blog data collection and curation. Section IV explains the data collected. In Section V, we demonstrate the importance of blog data analysis using Blogtrackers tool through a real-world case study. We conclude with intended future work in Section VI.

II. STATE OF THE ART

Despite the recent growth in the area of blog mining, several studies have been conducted to analyze how blog data can be effectively collected. Aschenbrenner and Miksch [14] study the development of mining techniques in a corporate environment. Their study shows a significant risk of failure due to the amount of open questions and misinformation currently available [14]. Tadanobu et al. analyzed various aspects of blog reading behavior [15]. The vast amounts of publicly available blogs have made it impossible to keep track of all of them [14]. Hence, there is a need for creating usable tools for extraction of vital information from the blogosphere.

There are some tools that were developed to analyze blogs data, but these attempts have been discontinued, such as: 1)*BlogPulse* which was developed by IntelliSeek. It was developed to provide search and analytic capabilities, automated web discovery for blogs, show the trends of information, and monitor the daily activity on weblogs. This tool was discontinued in 2012 [16][17]. 2)*Blogdex* was another service that has been discontinued; it provided a resource for understanding hot-button issues in the blogosphere. 3)*BlogScope*, was another blog tracking service developed as a research project in the department of computer science in university of Toronto, provided blog analytics and visualizations but was shut down in early 2012 [18][19]. 4)*Technorati* was originally launched as a blog index and search engine. It used a proprietary search and ranking algorithm to provide a rich directory of blogs sorted by content type and authority [20][21]. However, it did not provide blog monitoring or analytical capabilities to the end users. Furthermore, blog index and data is not available publicly to the researchers or practitioners community. The service now offers advertising platform to allow publishers to maximize their revenues without complications.

III. METHODOLOGY

To collect and store data, it is important to first identify a structure. After examining several blogs, we have identified a few common attributes such as: *title*, *author*, *date of posting*, *actual post*, *permalink*, and *number of comments* that almost all blogs have. We extract all these attributes while crawling each blog site.

For crawling blogs data, we setup crawler(s) for each blog site to extract all the required attributes. There are three main steps in crawling data from a blog site – (1) exploring the blog site, (2) crawling the blog site, and (3) cleaning and storing the data in a database for analysis and retrieval. Figure 1 shows the flow of the data crawling process.

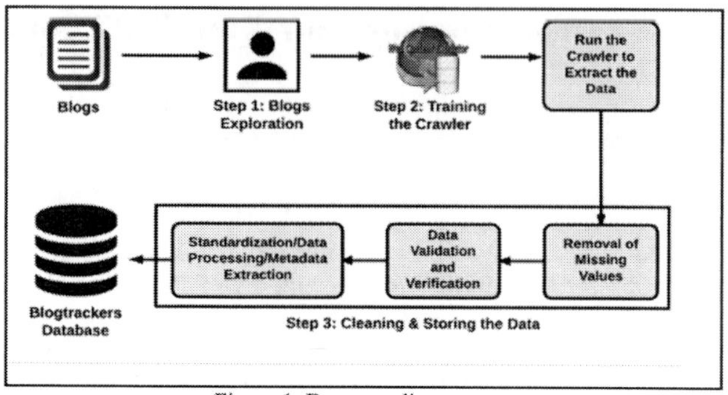

Figure 1: Data crawling process

A. *Exploring the blog site*

To train crawler(s) for a blog site, it is important to first study the structure of the blog site and understand the following:

- Type of blog site:
  - Blog on main stream media/journalist
  - Single author or multi-author blogs
  - Hobbyist blogger vs. professional blogger
  - Forum
- Site Owner(s)
- Sections of the site:
  - Archive
  - Topics or categories (e.g., news, entertainment, sports, politics, etc.)
- Language(s) of the site (inferred using AlchemyAPI [22])
- Web content structure:
  - Title of blog post
  - Author of blog post
  - Date of posting
  - Actual post/content of the post
  - Comments section
  - Tags
- Geographical location of the site (inferred using the IP address of the blog site's domain from Maltego [23])
- Description of the site
- Site navigation:
  - To identify next post or next page, if the blog is paginated
  - Search option for finding precise data.

These explorations will help us train our crawler to collect valid data and analyze them for gaining insights.

B. *Crawling the data*

Currently, we are using Web Content Extractor (WCE) tool for data collection. With this software, we train a crawler to extract data from blog sites efficiently. Figure 2 is a screenshot of the WCE.

To train the crawler, we first provide the starting or seed URLs. For example, the home page of a blog site or URL of the search page of a specific topic or section/s of a website. Then, we train the crawler to navigate to each blog post on the seed URLs as well as to the next page or older posts. Then, we take a sample post and define all the attributes we want to collect through WCE. Here, we need to carefully select the portion of the post to avoid noises. When all the attributes are selected, WCE is ready to run for collecting the data.

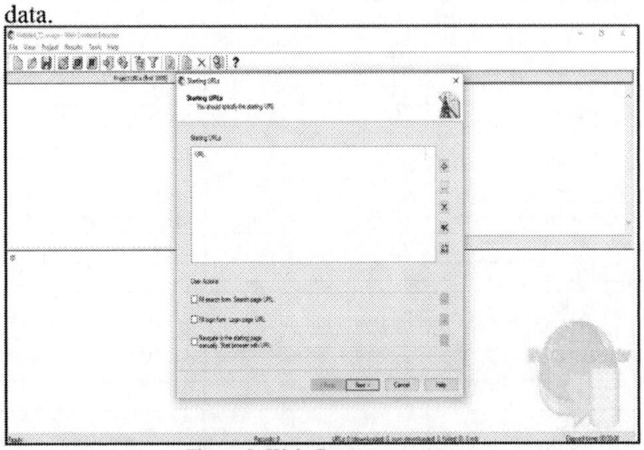

Figure 2: Web Content extractor

C. *Cleaning and Storing of Data*

Web crawling doesn't always give us clean data. It almost always crawls some noise. Data cleaning is required before using the data for analysis. For this, we follow a three-step cleaning process:

- Step 1- Cleaning from WCE: Deleting the empty fields and advertisement URLs. Later, the data is stored into a temporary database.
- Step 2- Cleaning by SQL Queries: Using SQL (Structured Query Language) to select validated and verified data from the temporary database. This step helps in removing the noise left unfiltered from previous step.
- Step 3- Cleaning by Script: In this step, a major part of cleaning along with data processing, metadata extraction, and data standardization is done. We exclude any possible noise and standardize attributes like date of posting. Followed by extracting metadata such as sentiments using LIWC (Linguistic Inquiry and Word Count) [24][25], outbound URLs, entities and their types, language of the post, proper author name etc. This is all performed before pushing the clean data into Blogtrackers database for analysis.

D. *Challenges*

Some of the challenges that we face during blog crawling process are:

- Changing blog structure – Blog site owners can change their blog structure any time and the crawler trained for one structure does not work for the other. This causes us to repeat the effort of training the crawler for the new structure of blog site.
- Noises – Irrespective of how well a crawler is trained, noise is always crawled. Social media plugins (such as Facebook share plugins, Twitter share plugins, etc.) and advertisements from the blog site could be crawled as JavaScript.
- Limitations of WCE – WCE sometimes fails to crawl dynamic pages that are loaded using JavaScript.

IV. DATA STATISTICS

Following the methodology proposed in Section III, we have crawled 194 blog sites, at the time of writing this paper and more blogs are being crawled. Blogs have been crawled for Ukraine-Russia Conflict, anti-NATO (the North Atlantic Treaty Organization) narratives, migrant crisis in the European Union, and the fake news blogs in the Baltic States. Below, we provide details for each dataset:

A. *Ukraine-Russia Conflict*

This blog dataset was collected from mid 2014 to mid 2016, during the political and military tension between Ukraine and Russia. A total of 57 blogs discussing the conflict were crawled. Tables 1 and 2 give location and language statistics for this dataset. Some blogs may have posts in more than one language.

TABLE 1. LOCATION DISTRIBUTION

Location	Blogs	Blog Posts
USA	43	15145
RUS	6	627
UKR	6	157
GBR	1	25
FRA	1	20

TABLE 2. LANGUAGE DISTRIBUTION

Language	Blogs	Blog Posts
English	42	15357
Russian	6	233
Danish	3	4
Spanish	2	9
Italian	2	2
Ukrainian	2	2
Swedish	1	45
Croatian	1	19
Norwegian	1	1
Polish	1	1
Portuguese	1	1
French	1	1

TABLE 3. LOCATION DISTRIBUTION

Location	Blogs	Blog Posts
USA	51	51436
RUS	4	3187
DEU	4	1609
NLD	3	5579
FRA	2	174
SVK	1	285
SRB	1	36
IRL	1	26
POL	1	16

UKR	1	6
ZWE	1	1

B. *Anti-NATO*

NATO's support of Ukraine during the Ukraine-Russia conflict caused an increase in the anti NATO narratives in the blogs and this sentiment was also observed during various exercises conducted by NATO (such as, Trident Juncture 2015, Brilliant Jump 2016, and Anakonda 2016). We crawled 70 blogs that had an anti-NATO propaganda from mid 2015 to late 2016. Tables 3 and 4 give statistics for this dataset.

TABLE 4. LANGUAGE DISTRIBUTION

Language	Blogs	Blog Posts
English	62	51467
French	16	223
Spanish	14	1542
German	13	1389
Russian	11	605
Polish	10	2228
Italian	9	449
Romanian	5	287
Danish	5	8
Catalan	4	104
Arabic	4	101
Czech	3	11
Finnish	3	6
Portuguese	3	4
Ukrainian	2	42
Afrikaans	2	9
Swahili	2	3
Dutch	2	3
Serbian	2	3
Welsh	2	3
Turkish	2	2
Croatian	1	1704
Greek	1	25
Basque	1	6
Hungarian	1	2
Albanian	2	2
Central mam	1	2
Faroese	1	2
Maltese	1	1
Indonesian	1	1
Tagalog	1	1
Slovak	1	1
Latvian	1	1

C. *EU migrant crisis*

Due to the conflict in Eastern Europe and Middle East during late 2015 and 2016, many people were migrating from war torn regions to stable regions in Europe. This dataset was collected in early 2016 during the height of migrant crisis in Europe. Tables 5 and 6 give statistics for this dataset.

TABLE 5. LOCATION DISTRIBUTION

Location	Blogs	Blog Posts
USA	21	9002
DEU	1	181

TABLE 6. LANGUAGE DISTRIBUTION

Language	Blogs	Blog Posts
English	22	7996
German	3	3
Greek	2	1039
Italian	1	4
Albanian	1	3
Croatian	1	3
Danish	1	2
Fulfulde Adamawa	1	2
Portuguese	1	2
Serbian	1	2
Czech	1	1
Finnish	1	1
Hawaiian	1	1
Polish	1	1
Turkish	1	1
Afrikaans	1	1
Hungarian	1	1
Dutch	1	1
Latin	1	1
Spanish	1	1

D. *Fake News Blogs in Baltic States*

There is a rising concern for fake news. Subject matter experts had identified 26 fake news blogs from the Baltic States, especially of Latvian, Estonian or Lithuanian origin suspected for disseminating fake news. We crawled 16667 blog posts from 21 blogs. This dataset was collected in early 2017. Tables 7 and 8 give basic statistics for this dataset.

TABLE 7. LOCATION DISTRIBUTION

Location	Blogs	Blog Posts
EST	7	2592
DEU	5	2156
LVA	3	1976
USA	3	3156
LTU	2	6595
NLD	1	192

TABLE 8. LANGUAGE DISTRIBUTION

Language	Blogs	Blog Posts
Latvian	10	3793
English	8	738
Russian	7	4599

Estonian	6	809
Lithuanian	2	6590
Bulgarian	1	1

V. DATA ANALYSIS

Blogs provide immense amount of content that can be analyzed to extract insights and sometimes gain situational awareness during conflicts. In this section, we explain the importance of analyzing blog data by extracting insights from our in-house developed tool, Blogtrackers (available for public use [13]).

We used Blogtrackers to understand the anti-NATO narratives disseminated in blogs during the NATO's Trident Juncture exercise conducted in October 2015. We started exploring our anti-NATO blogs dataset by studying the posting trends for the year 2015. Figure 3 is the posting frequency chart generated by Blogtrackers for the said period. We observed an increase in activity during August 2015 – December 2015, roughly 2 months before and after the exercise.

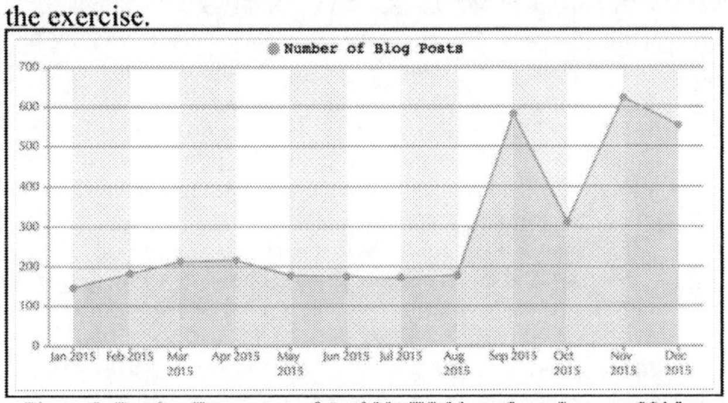

Figure 3: Posting Frequency of Anti-NATO blogs from January 2015 to December 2015.

We generated sentiment trends to understand the overall tonality of the bloggers' postings during this period. Figure 4 is the sentiment trend generated by Blogtrackers for the said period. We found that the sentiment was majorly positive up until the exercise, i.e., October 2015, and negative after the exercise, demonstrating that bloggers did not see the exercise in a good light. There was a strong anti-NATO sentiment stemming from anti-NATO propaganda.

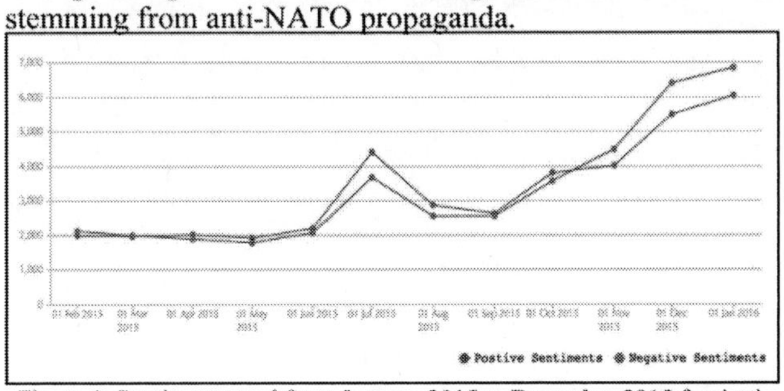

Figure 4: Sentiment trend from January 2015 to December 2015 for Anti-NATO blogs

We also generated the influence trend to understand the variation of blogger's influence over the community. This is helpful to know how the narratives in blogosphere resonated with the readers. Influence score for each blog post is based on the chatter it generates in the blogosphere. It is computed using the amount of discussion it generated (comments) and outbound URLs [26][27]. Influence of a blogger is assessed by how influential his/her posts are. Figure 5 is the influence trend of the top 5 (influential) bloggers in the said period.

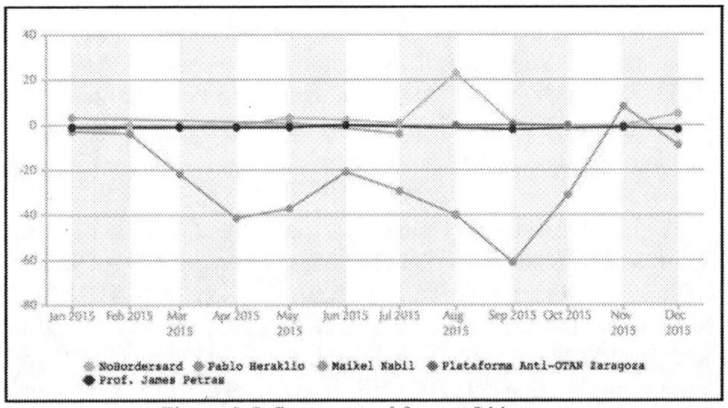

Figure 5: Influence trend for top 5 bloggers

Figure 6: Blog browser showing the most influential blog post.

From the trend chart in Figure 5, we identified NoBordersard was the most influential. As depicted in Figure 6, we used blog browser feature of Blogtrackers to know what has influenced the community. We found a blog post written by NoBordersard in Italian was calling for civil disobedience march against the NATO exercise. This blog post generated a considerable amount of chatter and had the highest influence.

VI. CONCLUSION AND FUTURE WORK

This article presents a novel approach on blog data collection. Currently, the approach followed is to - manually collect, clean and save blog data to relational databases for further analysis. This is helpful in many ways to benefit the user with the process of carefully analyzing the blog site structure and its changing nature, noises, and myriad other challenges. Obtaining a cleaner blog data sample is an extremely time consuming process and involves significant human intervention. Understandably, this is not a scalable approach, given the speed with which the blogosphere is expanding. Therefore, we are developing an automated crawling mechanism to overcome the challenges presented by blog data collection thereby significantly increasing the efficiency of the overall process from data to decisions.

The article also presented a case study on how Blogtrackers, tool for analyzing blogs, had sift through more than 60,000 blog posts from 70 anti-NATO blogs to identify a blog post calling for civil disobedience, explaining the significance of studying blogs in analyzing information dissemination through social media to identify blogs and bloggers calling for deviant activities. Going further, we would like to add content analysis features to Blogtrackers, such as: topic modeling, network analysis, and cyber forensics features, to not only study blogs individually, but also to understand their coordination structure and information dissemination structure.

ACKNOWLEDGMENT

This research is funded in part by the U.S. Nation Science Foundation (IIS-1110868 and ACI-1429160), U.S. Office of Naval Research (N000141010091, N000141410489, N0001415P1187, N000141612016, and N000141612412), U.S. Air Force Research Lab, U.S. Army Research Office (W911NF-16-1-0189), U.S. Defense Advanced Research Projects Agency (W31P4Q-17-C-0059) and the Jerry L. Maulden/Entergy Fund at the University of Arkansas at Little Rock. Any opinions, findings, and conclusions or recommendations expressed in this material are those of the authors and do not necessarily reflect the views of the funding organizations. The researchers gratefully acknowledge the support.

REFERENCES

[1] T. O'Reilly, "What is Web 2.0 - design patterns and business models for the next generation of software," 30-Sep-2005. [Online]. Available: http://www.oreilly.com/pub/a/web2/archive/what-is-web-20.html. [Accessed: 18-May-2017].

[2] D. Gillmor, "*We the media: Grassroots journalism by the people, for the people*", O'Reilly Media, Inc., 2006.

[3] "Stats — WordPress.com." [Online]. Available: https://wordpress.com/activity/. [Accessed: 04-Apr-2017].

[4] R. Scoble and S. Israel, "*Naked conversations: how blogs are changing the way businesses talk with customers*", John Wiley & Sons, 2006.

[5] M. Richardson and P. Domingos, "Mining knowledge-sharing sites for viral marketing," in *Proceedings of the eighth ACM SIGKDD international conference on Knowledge discovery and data mining*, New York, NY, USA, 2002, pp. 61–70.

[6] D. Gruhl, R. Guha, R. Kumar, J. Novak, and A. Tomkins, "The predictive power of online chatter," in *Proceedings of the eleventh ACM SIGKDD international conference on Knowledge discovery in data mining*, New York, NY, USA, 2005, pp. 78–87.

[7] G. Mishne and M. de Rijke, "Deriving wishlists from blogs show us your blog, and we'll tell you what books to buy," in *Proceedings of the 15th international conference on World Wide Web*, New York, NY, USA, 2006, pp. 925–926.

[8] T. R. Coffman and S. E. Marcus, "Dynamic classification of groups through social network analysis and hmms," in *Aerospace Conference, 2004. Proceedings. 2004 IEEE*, 2004, vol. 5, pp. 3197–3205.

[9] M. Thelwall, "Bloggers during the London attacks: Top information sources and topics," in *Proceedings of the 3rd International Workshop on the Weblogging Ecosystem (WWE 2006)*, 2006.

[10] S. Al-khateeb, M. Hussain, and N. Agarwal, "Analyzing Deviant Socio-technical Behaviors using Social Network Analysis and Cyber Forensics-based Methodologies," in *Big Data Analytics in Cybersecurity and IT Management*, CRC Press, Taylor & Francis, in press.

[11] S. Al-khateeb and N. Agarwal, "Understanding Strategic Information Maneuvers in Network Media to Advance Cyber Operations: A Case Study Analyzing pro-Russian separatisits' Cyber Information Operations in Crimean Water Crisis," *J. Balt. Secur.*, vol. 2, no. 1, pp. 6–27, 2016.

[12] J. Kopecky, N. Bos, and A. Greenberg, "Social identity modeling: past work and relevant issues for socio-cultural modeling," in *Proceedings of the 19th Conference on Behavior Representation in Modeling and Simulation, Charleston, SC*, 2010, pp. 203–210.

[13] "Blogtrackers." [Online]. Available: http://blogtrackers.host.ualr.edu/. [Accessed: 18-May-2017].

[14] A. Aschenbrenner and S. Miksch, "Blog mining in a corporate environment," *Vienna Univ. Technol. Inst. Softw. Technol. Interact. Syst. Res. Studio Austria Smart Agent Technol.*, 2005.

[15] T. Furukawa, M. Ishizuka, Y. Matsuo, I. Ohmukai, K. Uchiyama, and others, "Analyzing reading behavior by blog mining," in *Proceedings of the National Conference on Artificial Intelligence*, 2007, vol. 22, p. 1353.

[16] M. Hurst, "Farewell To BlogPulse | SmartData Collective," *SmartData Collective*, 14-Jan-2012. [Online]. Available: http://www.smartdatacollective.com/matthewhurst/44748/farewell-blogpulse. [Accessed: 18-May-2017].

[17] "BlogPulse," *Wikipedia*. 08-Mar-2017.

[18] N. Bansal and N. Koudas, "Blogscope: a system for online analysis of high volume text streams," in *Proceedings of the 33rd international conference on Very large data bases*, 2007, pp. 1410–1413.

[19] "BlogScope," *Wikipedia*. 29-Nov-2015.

[20] "Technorati—the World's Largest Blog Directory—is Gone," *Business 2 Community*. [Online]. Available: http://www.business2community.com/social-media/technorati-worlds-largest-blog-directory-gone-0915716. [Accessed: 04-Apr-2017].

[21] "About Us | Technorati." [Online]. Available: http://technorati.com/company/about-us/. [Accessed: 18-May-2017].

[22] "AlchemyAPI," *Wikipedia*. 02-May-2017.

[23] "Paterva Home." [Online]. Available: https://www.paterva.com/web7/. [Accessed: 18-May-2017].

[24] I. LIWC, "Linguistic Inquiry and Word Count (LIWC)." [Online]. Available: www.liwc.wpengine.com. [Accessed: 12-Apr-2016].

[25] J. W. Pennebaker, M. E. Francis, and R. J. Booth, "Linguistic inquiry and word count: LIWC 2001," *Mahway Lawrence Erlbaum Assoc.*, vol. 71, no. 2001, p. 2001, 2001.

[26] N. Agarwal, H. Liu, L. Tang, and S. Y. Philip, "Modeling blogger influence in a community," *Soc. Netw. Anal. Min.*, vol. 2, no. 2, pp. 139–162, 2012.

[27] N. Agarwal, D. Mahata, and H. Liu, "Time- and Event-Driven Modeling of Blogger Influence," in *Encyclopedia of Social Network Analysis and Mining*, R. Alhajj and J. Rokne, Eds. New York, NY: Springer New York, 2014, pp. 2154–2165.

A New Graph-Based Approach for Document Similarity Using Concepts of Non-Rigid Shapes

Lorena Castillo Galdos[1], Grimaldo Dávila Guillén[1], Cristian López Del Alamo[1,2]
[1]Universidad Nacional de San Agustín, [2]Universidad La Salle
Computer Science
Arequipa, Perú
e-mail:lcastillo@unsa.edu.pe, gdavila@unsa.edu.pe, clopez@ulasalle.edu.pe

***Abstract*—Most methods used to compare text documents are based on the space vector model; however, this model does not capture the relations between words, which is considered necessary to make better comparisons. In this research, we propose a method based on the creation of graphs to get semantic relations between words and we adapt algorithms of the theory of non-rigid 3D model analysis.**

Keywords-document similarity; keypoints; keywords; graph based comparison; non rigid shapes

I. INTRODUCTION

The development of technology and, specifically, of the Internet and storage devices, has grown exponentially in the last years, providing a great quantity of textual information, but also generating new challenges. For instance, some of these challenges include document analysis based on the document structure grammar, plagiarism detection, text content search, and others. These problems are converted into areas of interest in the community of Information Retrieval.

As a consequence, in the last years, investigations to generate algorithms for information retrieval by content have been developed. One of the most common methods is the vector-space model [4]; however, this approach does not capture the semantic relations between documents.

On the other hand, in the last years, many algorithms applied to similitude search in non-rigid three-dimensional models have been developed. These algorithms have the advantage of retrieving similar topology three-dimensional models; i.e. they are invariant to non-rigid transformations, like isometric changes and noise presence, among others.

Furthermore, there are many areas in computer science that can provide some ideas and concepts that can be applied to information retrieval. For instance, three-dimensional models and documents can be treated like graphs; then, graph theory based algorithms may be used to analyze the existence of isomorphism patterns and semantic similitudes between the objects.

There are three main contributions of this paper. First, we apply concepts of three-dimensional invariant models such as key-points and K-rings, which are adapted to generate an algorithm for semantic document comparison. Second, we introduce a new form of creating document keypoints-based graphs, and finally, we propose a new approach for key-point comparison in text graph representation.

The rest of this paper is organized as follows. In Section 2, the related work is presented. In section 3, we show the concepts of keypoint and document analysis adapted key components. Section 4 describes the proposal and methodology applied in this research. Section 5 shows the experiments and evaluations and, finally, Section 6 presents the conclusions.

II. RELATED WORK

There exist works in the literature in which graphs are used to compare and classify documents [7][8][11]. The creation and use of text graphs may vary according to their application. These can be term graphs, document graphs, and category graphs, among others.

When we make a semantic comparison between documents, the entered data or the documents itself may change; so, the output data and the techniques must also change. For this reason, Pilehvar et al. [8] proposed a graph based unified approach for measuring the semantic similarity and a multiple-level item comparison. Namely, they proposed sense, words and text levels.

Similarly, in [7] a document is represented as a compact concept graph. Here, the nodes represent extracted concepts from the document and the edges represent the semantic and structural relations between them, which are used to measure the semantic similarity between documents.

To measure the similarity between documents in a category, Wang et al. [11] propose the generation of a term graph. The objective is to represent the document content and the relation between words in order to define new functions of graph-based similarity. This allows combining the advantages of the vector-space model and o-occurring terms (*frequent itemset mining method* [6]).

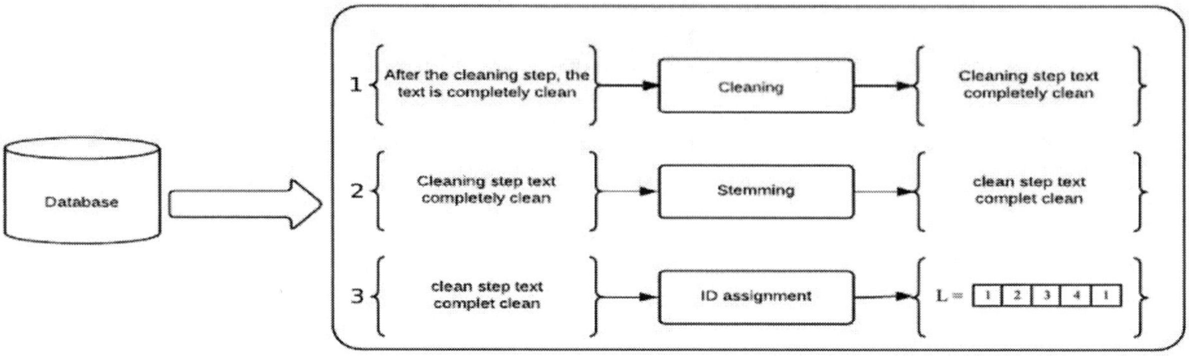

Figure. 1. Preprocessing

In [1], neighboring document graphs are generated in one hyperlink space, in which the nodes are the Web pages, and the edges are the hyperlinks between them, which helps with the task of classifying and labeling each category.

Unlike previous research papers that focus on creating maximum co-occurrence graphs and word frequency based graphs, we concentrate on determining keywords. These words are the ones that not only have high frequency but also have a strong relation inside a word neighborhood. This concept is taken from the term keypoints [5] used in non-rigid three-dimensional models, aiming to determine high curvature localized vertices. With this, a 3D model with 10 000 vertices is reduced to a small subset if these vertices represent high semantic sense zones of the three-dimensional model. Similarly, in this paper, we propose to determine a set of keywords that represent high semantic content zones of the document.

In the next section, we specify the concepts of keypoints and k-rings and their respective adaptations to the information retrieval field.

III. PRELIMINARY CONCEPTS

A. *Keypoints and Keywords*

In 3D models, a keypoint is a point that holds some distinctive characteristics inside its neighborhood and it is present in different object instances [5].

On the other hand, in a similar way, the keywords (kw) of a document are defined as the words that bring more semantic information about a set of neighbor words. So, its frequency is high, and at the same time, the degree in which this keyword is related to its neighbors is seen many times in the document.

B. *K-rings and Neighborhood*

In 3D models a k-ring $R_k(v)$of k profundity level with center on the vertex v is defined by:

$$R_k(v) = \{v' \in V', | C(v',v) | = k\} \quad (1)$$

where $C(v',v)$ is the shortest path from vertex v' to v and $|C(v',v)|$, is the size of the path $C(v',v)$. It is important to mention that the size of an edge is always 1 [3].

The adapted concept of k-ring for documents is called neighborhood. The neighborhood of a node n iscomposed of all the nodes inside a radius ρ having the center on the node n which has to exist in both graphs to be compared.

IV. METHODOLOGY

In this section, we describe the necessary stages to obtain the most relevant characteristics of a document using adapted techniques of similarity search in non-rigid three-dimensional models. These stages are divided into three phases. The first stage, named preprocessing stage, is summarized in Fig. 1 and described in the next subsection. The second stage is called graph construction and finally, the third stage is graph comparison.

A. *Preprocessing*

1. **Cleaning**: Because not all the words in the document bring relevant information (like *stop words*), it is required to eliminate them, and usually these are the most frequent, for example: pronouns, articles, etc.
2. **Stemming**: One of the problems that occur in natural language is that a word can have different variations of time, gender, and number; these variations affect the computational calculation because a word represented differently can be interpreted in a different manner, namely, as two separate nodes in the graph. To avoid this problem, we use the Porter [9] algorithm, which allows us to make a stemming process, and hence obtain the roots of the words after the cleaning process.
3. **ID Assignment:** We manage to handle the roots in a different manner, assigning a unique numeric identifier to each root (ID), to insert them later in a list L, which will contain all the roots' IDs of the document in the occurrence order in the text.

$$L = \{ id_1, id_2, ..., id_t\} \quad (2)$$

where id_i is the *id* of the word in the position i. For example, if the word *friend* has the $id = 5$, then all the occurrences of the word friend in the text will have the $id = 5$. This identifier is assigned with the objective of handling the term graph with integer numbers instead of words, and to accelerate the comparison algorithm between edges or vertices. Finally, t represents the number of words of the text after the cleaning process.

B. *Graph construction*

After the preprocessing stage, we build the graph $G(N, A, W)$ where N are the nodes of the graph, which represent the elements of the list L, i.e., the representative words of the text. Set A indicates the edges, which represent the relations that exist between the elements of the list L, and set W the weights of each edge; this weight accounts for the degree of importance of that relation.

The protruding edges of a node N_i represent the degree in which this node is related to its neighbor nodes. That is, the degree in which a word is related to adjacent words in the text. This degree is represented by the value $K >= 1$ as it is shown in Fig. 2.

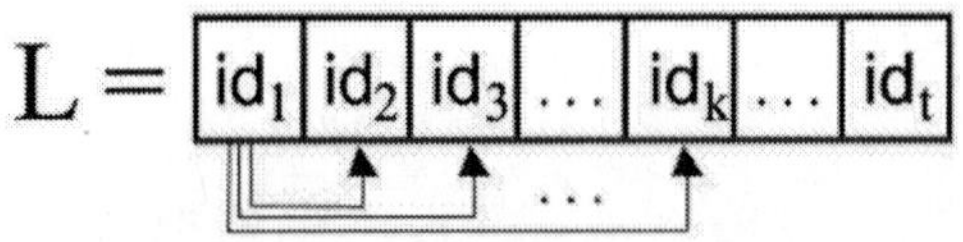

Figure. 2. Degree K in the list L

In equation (3), we formally describe the edges A of the graph $G(N, A, W)$:

$$A = \{l_i l_{i+1}[w_{i,i+1}], \ldots, l_i l_k[w_{i,k}]\} \quad 1 <= i <= s \qquad (3)$$

where w_{ij} is the weight between the edge i and the edge j, $i < j < k$, l_i is an element of the list L and s is the number of edges in the graph.

To each node, we assigned a weight ψ that will be the summation of the weights of the adjacent edges of the node; this can be observed in Fig. 3 b), which will serve to determine the keywords in the text.

C. *Comparison*

In the comparison stage, we obtain the keywords (kw) of the compared graphs.

Let G_1 and G_2 be two graphs that represent two documents. Then, the keywords of G_1 and G_2 are those μ nodes whose weights are the maximum. In other words, if we order all the vertices of G_1 and G_2 decreasingly and take the first μ nodes of both lists, then we have the keywords of both graphs.

Then, we find the intersection of both lists, so that the nodes with more weight, that are both in G_1 and G_2 will be the set of common keywords between both graphs. This can be represented formally in (4).

$$KW(G_1, G_2) = max_\mu(G_1) \cap max_\mu(G_2)\} \qquad (4)$$

where max_μ represent the μ higher values, G_1 and G_2 are the graphs that represent two different documents, and finally $KW(G_1, G_2)$ is the set of common keywords between $G_1$and G_2.

On the other hand, considering that an edge represents the relation between two words *(a,b)* of the text T, and its weight w is the number of times this *(a,b)* relation is repeated in the document, to find the distance or dissimilarity between two graphs, we propose to use the inverse of the weights of the edge w so we can get the distance between two graphs. This is shown in (5).

$$D_{a,b} = \{\frac{1}{w_{a,b}}\} \qquad (5)$$

In Fig 3 a), a graph is shown, where the vertices represent the words, and the vertices labels are the *ids* of those words. On the other hand, the edges represent the relations between neighbor words, and their respective labels are the number of times that the relationship appears in the document.

For each node, we calculate the sum of the weights of the protruding edges, as we can observe in Fig. 3 b); so that, the higher the value of one node, the greater the strength of the relations it maintains with its neighbors. So, a node with a higher value is probably a word of high importance in the text.

Finally, as it is shown in Fig. 3 c), the weights of the edges have been inverted according to (5), so we can apply the Dijkstra algorithm and find the neighborhood of a vertex v inside a ρ radius.

To find the keypoints, we must consider the neighborhood inside a ρ radius of a node, and, as we can see in Fig. 4 a), v is the key point from which the k-rings will be taken. The color nodes represent the neighbors of v, and each color represents a different neighborhood. In Fig. 4 b), the concept of k-rings is adapted, so that ρ represents the radius and all the nodes inside of it are the neighborhood of the node n.

In Fig. 5, we apply the Dijkstra algorithm to the graphs $G_1$and G_2 for comparison. We do this to obtain the minimum distance from the nodes of the list L_{kw} and the rest of the nodes in both graphs, as shown in Fig. 5 a) and 5 b).

Next, based on the idea of [2], (6) formally describes the way of finding the neighborhood, which is the disjoint union ⊔, of the intersections of the adjacent nodes to the keywords inside a ρ radius.

$$R = \{F\rho(L_{kw_1}) \sqcup \ldots \sqcup F\rho(L_{kw_{|L_{kw}|}})\} \qquad (6)$$

where $F\rho(L_{kw_j}) = \{n \in G_1, G_2 : D(n, L_{kw_j}) <= \rho\}$, D denotes the shortest distance between the node n and L_{kw_j}through the Dijkstra algorithm, n are all the nodes whose distance D is less than a radius ρ, as shown in Fig. 5.

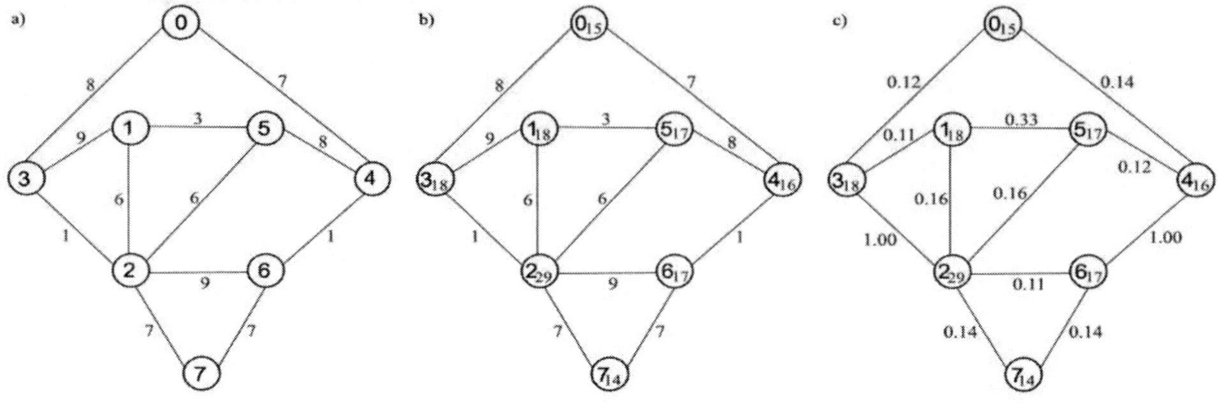

Figure 3. Weighted Graph G1

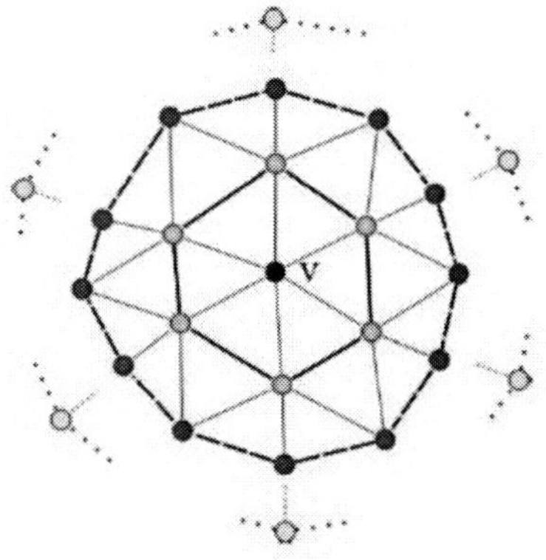

a) k-rings [10]

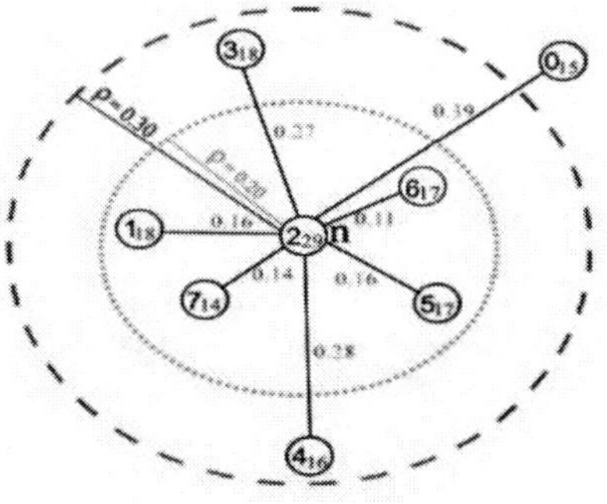

b) *radius* ρ

Fig. 4. Comparison between a K-ring centered on a vertex v of a 3D model triangular mesh, and a K-ring in a document, with a neighborhood ρ

We defined the coefficient of C as:

$$C = |R| + |L_{kw}| \quad (7)$$

where $|R|$ represents the importance of the relation between words and $|L_{kw}|$represents the importance of the individuality of these. Finally, the coefficient of similarity S is defined as:

$$S = \begin{cases} \text{if } C = 0, \text{ inf} \\ \text{if } C > 0, 1/C \end{cases} \quad (8)$$

V. EXPERIMENTS AND RESULTS

The experiments were conducted using the *Reuters-21578* database, from which we chose the documents of the top 10 categories. The categories and the number of documents per category used in the experiments are listed in Table I. These documents were preprocessed according to the subsection IV-A of Section IV. Then, for each document, the corresponding graph was created, as indicated subsection IV-B. Finally, after applying the graph comparison method proposed in subsection IV-C, we made comparisons between the graphs to obtain a similarity matrix, to which we applied a minimum spanning tree algorithm to detect the groups with similar documents.

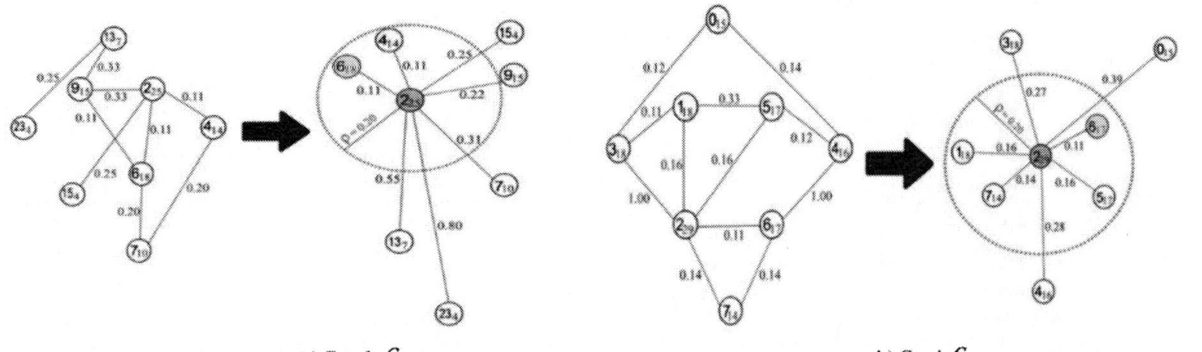

a) *Graph* G_1 b) Graph G_2

Figure 5. $F_{0.02}(2) = \{6\}$

TABLE I. TOP 10 REUTERS-21578 CATEGORIES

Category	Number of Documents
acq	2131
corn	209
crude	512
earn	3754
grain	529
interest	391
money-fx	603
ship	277
trade	450
wheat	264

In addition, once we get the minimum spanning tree, we take all pairs of adjacent nodes of the tree, and we value the categories they have in common. If two nodes have a category Z in common, then both belong to this category Z. Finally, the groups generated with the real categories of the Reuters-21578 database are contrasted.

In Table II, we can observe the results in each experiment. In the table, we can appreciate that the experiment with the less number of keywords kw = *5* and the less number of radius ρ=1, column 3 in the table, obtains the worst results. On the other hand, incrementing the number of kw to 10, and the radius ρ to 2, improves the percentage of documents correctly classified. However, if we perform a high increment in the kw number, for example, 15 and the radius ρ of 2, the percentage of success decreases, as we can see in column 7 of Table II.

In Fig. 6, we can observe the results of applying the minimum spanning tree algorithm to the matrix of document similarity. Different colors represent different categories.

VI. CONCLUSIONS

In this research, we presented an algorithm for document similarity based on concepts from the non-rigid three-dimensional model analysis. The proposed algorithm presented average results of 85% to 90% correctly classified documents. Nevertheless, when considering a major number of keywords and radius, the quality of the documents properly classified decreases; this can be because of the size of the text. In Reuters-21578 database, the size of the text is small and thus, the number of keywords and the neighborhood radius must also be short. On the other hand, as the radius increments, the number of representative key points decreases, which has an adverse effect on the document classification.

In future works, the comparisons will be made with other techniques using large text databases, because it is expected that with larger amount of text, the detection of keywords will be improved. Finally, it is possible to join different nodes from the document graph where each node represents equal words (synonyms), in order to improve the process of comparison.

REFERENCES

[1] R. Angelova and G. Weikum, "Graph-based text classification: learn from your neighbors". In *Proceedings of the 29th annual international ACM SIGIR conference on Research and development in information retrieval* , pp. 485-492. ACM, 2006.

[2] E. Boyer, A. M. Bronstein, M. M. Bronstein, B.Bustos, T. Darom, R. Horaud, I. Hotz, Y. Keller, J. Keustermans, A. Kovnatsky, et al. Shrec 2011: robust feature detection and description benchmark. *arXiv preprint arXiv:1102.4258*, 2011.

[3] C. J. L. Del Alamo, L. A. R. Calla, and L. J. F. Perez, "Efficient approach for interest points detection in non-rigid shapes," in *Computing Conference (CLEI), 2015 Latin American*, pp. 1-8. IEEE, 2015.

[4] S. Dominich. *Mathematical foundations of information retrieval*, vol. 12. Springer Science & Business Media, 2012.

[5] H. Dutagaci, C. P. Cheung, and A. Godil. "Evaluation of 3d interest point detection techniques via human-generated ground truth". *The Visual Computer*, 28(9):901-917, 2012.

[6] B. Liu, C. W. Chin, and H. T. Ng. "Mining topic-specific concepts and definitions on the web". In *Proceedings of the 12th international conference on World Wide Web*, pp. 251-260. ACM, 2003.

[7] Y. Ni, Q. K. Xu, F. Cao, Y. Mass, D. Sheinwald, H. J. Zhu,

and S. S. Cao. "Semantic documents relatedness using concept graph representation". In *Proceedings of the Ninth ACM International Conference on Web Search and Data Mining*, pp.635-644. ACM, 2016.

[8] M. T. Pilehvar and R. Navigli. "From senses to texts: An all- in-one graph-based approach for measuring semantic similarity". *Artificial Intelligence*, 228:95-128, 2015.

[9] M. F. Porter. "An algorithm for suffix stripping". *Program*, 14(3):130-137, 1980.

[10] I. Sipiran and B. Bustos. "Harris 3d: a robust extension of the harris operator for interest point detection on 3d meshes". *The Visual Computer*, 27(11):963-976, 2011.

[11] W. Wang, D. B. Do, and X. Lin. "Term graph model for text classification". In *Advanced Data Mining and Applications*, pp.19-30. Springer, 2005.

TABLE II. EXPERIMENT RESULTS WITH ROUNDED PERCENTAGE, USING DIFFERENT NUMBER OF KEYWORDS, DEGREE OF ADJACENCY AND RADIUS

Category	**Total**	**kw = 5** $\rho = 1$	**kw = 5** $\rho = 3$	**kw = 10** $\rho = 1$	**kw = 10** $\rho = 2$	**kw = 15** $\rho = 4$
acq	2131	87%	91%	91%	92%	91%
corn	209	74%	79%	78%	78%	80%
crude	512	88%	90%	88%	90%	93%
earn	3754	97%	98%	98%	98%	98%
grain	529	88%	92%	91%	91%	92%
interest	391	84%	86%	85%	87%	86%
money-fx	603	90%	92%	90%	92%	90%
ship	277	78%	81%	78%	81%	87%
trade	450	87%	90%	88%	90%	90%
wheat	264	82%	83%	84%	81%	83%

Figure. 6. Minimum spanning tree of results after applying the Kruskall algorithm in the matrix of results with test of $kw = 5$, $\rho = 3$ and adjacency $k = 1$, each color represents one of the 10 categories.

Improving Twitter Sentiment Classification Using Term Usage and User Based Attributes

Selim Akyokuş[1], Murat Can Ganiz[2], Cem Gümüş[3]
Dogus University[1], Marmara University[2], Dogus University[3]
Istanbul, Turkey
e-mail: sakyokus@dogus.edu.tr[1], murat.ganiz@marmara.edu.tr[2], 201091001@dogus.edu.tr[3]

Abstract—**With the rapid growth of the Internet and the increase in the use of mobile devices, social media has grown rapidly in recent years. Without using appropriate representation techniques, processing methods and algorithms, it is difficult to get patterns, trends and opinions that are of interest to companies, organizations and individuals. Sentiment classification, which is one of the most popular mining tasks on the textual part of the social media data, aims to classify comment texts by their polarity. Textual features such as terms, n-grams combined with the NLP techniques are commonly used for this task. Our aim in this study is to see the effect of additional features on Twitter sentiment classification that are extracted from structured data related to the tweets and the Twitter users associated with these tweets. In addition to the use of terms in tweets as features i.e. traditional bag-of-words model, we employed tweet term usage based attributes along with Twitter user based attributes and showed that these additional attributes increase the accuracy of class substantially.**

Keywords-component; Sentiment Analysis; Sentiment Classification; Machine Learning; Feature Engineering; Feature Extraction;

I. INTRODUCTION

People's desire to share ideas, opinions and suggestions using social media has enabled the collection of huge amounts of data on the Internet. The raw data kept in social media environments must be preprocessed, represented, and analyzed in order to extract important patterns and trends. Typos, heavy use of slang, abbreviations, emotional expressions and the use of informal - daily conversation language make it difficult to work on the textual part of the social media data.

Twitter is one of the most widely used social media environments that have attracted many researchers for sentiment analysis. Sentiment analysis on Twitter data is more difficult than traditional textual documents due to characteristics of Twitter data. Twitter allows users to post messages of at most 140 characters. Because of this limitation, users tend to abbreviate words, use special characters and acronyms. The majority of messages are about current news and events in a conversional style. Although Twitter messages are short, the number of messages and different terms used in messages about a topic can be very high. This causes high dimensionality and sparsity on Twitter data sets.

The Twitter system allows researchers to collect tweets by using publicly available Application Programming Interfaces (APIs). Using the API, tweets about specified keywords and phrases can be obtained as a stream. Many studies have been done on Twitter messages by collecting data with this API. Examples of these studies include studies predicting outbreaks [1], examining medications and their unknown side effects [2], estimating changes in human perception over time [3], and perceptual analysis on the tweets of tourists coming to a tourist destination [4]. In the field of emotion analysis, although there are many studies for Twitter data written in English [5]-[8], a limited number of studies have been done for Turkish [9][10].

In this study, firstly data was collected from Twitter with a custom crawler application. The Web application was developed for data labelling. Tweets were shown to Dogus University students by this application. Of these tweets, all content is only in Turkish were labeled by the Dogus University students. After this, we preprocessed the labeled Twitter data. The preprocessing step included removal of stopwords, normalization of some terms, tokenization, and formation of term-document (tweet) matrix with Term Frequency-Inverse Document Frequency (TF-IDF) [18] weighting. We also computed several term and user statistics as additional features to be added to the term-document matrix. The additional features included user tweet counts and tweet term usage rate information. Balanced and unbalanced data sets were prepared with these collected data. Several classification algorithms from machine learning domain have been applied on to these datasets and the effects of the additional features have been investigated.

This paper is organized as follows: Section II presents general aspects of data preparation. In Section III, we show the results of experiments. Last Section summarizes our contribution.

II. DATA SET

A. Data collection and storage

To collect Twitter data, a Java application has been developed using Twitter API. This application obtained tweets written in all languages from the Twitter system. We collected tweets written in all languages. The collected

Twitter records were saved in the tables created in the PostgreSQL [13] relational database.

B. Data labelling

Data labelling manually is a tedious work and requires many people. That's why we chose students from our university. A Web application has been developed using the ZK framework [14], Spring framework [15], Hibernate [16] and Java [17] to label the collected data so that it can be used in classification. Tweets about Turkish companies operating in banking, telecom companies, universities and mobile phone device brands are shown to Dogus University students by the Web application. Of these tweets, mixed type of tweets were not labelled (e.g., half Turkish, half English). Only those all content is with Turkish were labeled by the students as positive, negative and neutral by using this application. Our study, each tweet labelled by a single student. Depending on the content of each tweet was labelled by students according their opinion and feelings. Within the scope of this study, 20204 tweets were labelled. Table I shows the number of labelled tweets.

- TT-BC: Tweets about banking.
- TT-TC: Tweets about telecom companies.
- TT-US: Tweets about universities.
- TT-PB: Tweets about mobile phone device brands.

TABLE I. LABELLED TWEET DETAILS

Tweet Topic	Type			
	Positive	Negative	Neutral	Total
TT-BC	1451	4603	1997	8051
TT-TC	2226	2738	884	5848
TT-US	1429	2230	1332	4991
TT-PB	586	322	406	1314
Total	**5692**	**9893**	**4619**	**20204**

C. Data preprocessing

There are some irrelevant terms and character sequences in Twitter messages that are not valuable or informative for classification tasks. Messages posted by Twitter users may include the following irrelevant terms.

- User names starting with "@" character ,
- Hashtags starting with "#" character ,
- Emotion expressions and
- URLs

Some data cleansing and preprocessing work were performed to remove these terms so that more effective results can be obtained in experiments. In addition, repeated messages shared by a person, messages containing only a URL, hashtag, special character, number and emotion expressions were deleted before the preprocessing steps. During the preprocessing step, Twitter messages about telecom companies were processed as described below.

1) Tokenize strings: It is a process that tries to tokenize messages and get meaningful data from them. The following operations have been applied:

- The URL, hashtag, usernames and special characters in the messages have been deleted.
- The contents of the messages have been converted to lowercase and all characters outside the letters have been deleted.

2) Stemming (Root finding): Stemming is a means for grouping words with a similar meaning together. In stemming, stemming algorithms transform inflected words to their word stem, or root form. For this purpose, the Zemberek library [12] was used to find the roots of Turkish words.

3) Correction of erroneous terms: It is a process that aims to correct terms that were mistakenly written in messages. The propositional function of the Zemberek library [12] was used for this process.

4) Deletion of repeated terms: It is a process that aims to reduce the size of characters and the correction of repetitive letters in the terms used in messages. In this study, repetitive letters in terms were deleted (e.g., Haapppyyyyy).

5) TF-IDF [18] weighting: In TF-IDF weighting scheme, a weight of each term in document is computed. Each weight represents the importance of a term inside a document [10]. TF-IDF was calculated for each term as follows:

$$TF(t,d) = 1 + \log_{10} f_d(t) \tag{1}$$

$$IDF(t,D) = \log_{10}\left(\frac{|D|}{df(t)}\right) \tag{2}$$

$$TF\text{-}IDF(t,d,D) = TF(t,d).\ IDF(t,D) \tag{3}$$

Where,

$f_d(t)$	: Frequency of term t in document (tweet)
d	: Document in corpus
$df(t)$	: The number of tweets that contain term t
D	: Corpus of documents (tweets)
$\|D\|$	: Total number of tweets in corpus

6) Calculation of tweet term usage statistics: Positive, negative, neutral and total tweet term usage rates were calculated for use in experiments. Equations about term statistics are our equations. The values calculated for each of these tweets were added as attributes to term-document matrix.

- The Tweet Term Usage Rate is calculated as follows (4):

$$WT(d_i) = \sum_{j=0}^{|d_i|} \log_{10} \frac{|DT|}{f_D(d_{i,j})} \quad (4)$$

Where,

$|DT|$: Total number of terms in corpus
d_i : Document (tweet) i in tweet corpus
$|d_i|$: The number of terms in document i
$d_{i,j}$: j^{th} term in document i
$f_D(t)$: Frequency of term t in all tweets in corpus

- The Tweet Term Positive Usage Rate is calculated as follows (5):

$$WP(d_i) = \sum_{j=0}^{|d_i|} \log_{10} \frac{|DP|}{f_{DP}(d_{i,j})} \quad (5)$$

Where,

$|DP|$: Total number of terms in positive tweets corpus
$f_{DP}(t)$: Frequency of term t in positive tweets in corpus

- The Tweet Term Negative Usage Rate is calculated as follows (6):

$$WN(d_i) = \sum_{j=0}^{|d_i|} \log_{10} \frac{|DN|}{f_{DN}(d_{i,j})} \quad (6)$$

Where,

$|DN|$: Total number of terms in negative tweets corpus
$f_{DN}(t)$: Frequency of term t in negative tweets in corpus

- The Tweet Term Neutral Usage Rate is calculated as follows (7):

$$WR(d_i) = \sum_{j=0}^{|d_i|} \log_{10} \frac{|DR|}{f_{DR}(d_{i,j})} \quad (7)$$

Where,

$|DR|$: Total number of terms in neutral tweets corpus
$f_{DR}(t)$: Frequency of term t in neutral tweets in corpus

7) Finding user statistics (tweet counts): Positive, negative, neutral and total tweet counts of users were calculated for use in experiments. The values calculated for each user have been added as attributes to term-document matrix.

$U_t(i)$: Total number of tweets posted by user i
$U_p(i)$: Total number of positive tweets posted by user i
$U_n(i)$: Total number of negative tweets posted user i
$U_r(i)$: Total number of neutral tweets posted by user i

D. Data Set Preparation

After data cleansing and preprocessing on tweets, several datasets were prepared by taking tweets about telecom companies for use in experiments. A Java [17] application has been developed to prepare data sets. Using this application, two types of data sets were created for the experiments: balanced and unbalanced. The classification on the balanced data set is more successful than expected. For this reason, we wanted to see the differences by preparing a balanced and unbalanced dataset. In balanced data sets, the number of instances in each class is the same. The number of instances in unbalanced data sets and the balanced data sets are shown in the Table II. In addition, we used four different representation methods:

- TF-IDF: Term-document matrix includes entries where each value is weighed using TF-IDF method.
- TF-IDF + US: User statistics features added to TF-IDF matrix
- TF-IDF + TS: Term statistics features are added to TF-IDF matrix
- TF-IDF + TS + US: Both term statistics and user statistics features are added to TF-IDF matrix.

TABLE II. DATA SET DETAILS

Data Set Type	Type			
	Positive	Negative	Neutral	Total
Unbalanced	1272	1140	504	2916
Balanced	504	504	504	1512

III. EXPERIMENTS

We used Weka [11] for sentiment classification with default Weka [11] parameters. Weka [11] is a widely used tool written in Java [17] for data mining research. It includes a collection of machine learning algorithms for data mining tasks. Naive Bayes Multinomial (NBM), Random Forest (RF), Sequential Minimal Optimization (SMO), Decision Tree (J48) and 1-Nearest Neighbors (IB1) algorithms [19]-[21] are used for sentiment classification in our experiments. 10-fold cross-validation and repeated holdout methods were used as accuracy estimation methods. In repeated holdout method, the data set was randomly separated 10 times into two sets: 80% for training and 20% for testing. Then, average accuracies of classifiers were computed using 10 tests.

The experiment with 10-fold cross validation on unbalanced data set is shown in Figure 1. The first row shows accuracies of different classification algorithms using only TF-IDF weighting method. In the second row, we added four features U_t, U_p, U_n and U_r involving user statistics to see their effects. The third row shows the effect of term statistics obtained by formulas (4)-(7). The last row (labeled TF-IDF + TS + US) displays the accuracies of algorithms the data set which includes TF-IDF weighting, term statistics and user statistics. Figure 2 shows accuracies of classifiers using repeated holdout method with 10 repetitions. The best performance results are obtained with decision tree (J48) and random forest algorithms. From the last two columns, we can observe that both user statistics and term statistics features increase the performances of classifiers. The best accuracy 71.70% is obtained by applying J48 algorithm on the data set that includes all TF-IDF weighting, term statistics and user statistics.

The experiment with 10-fold cross validation on balanced data set is shown in Figure 3. Figure 4 shows the results of experiments using repeated holdout method with 10 repetitions on balanced datasets. As it can be seen in Figures 3 and 4, balanced data sets produce better performance results than unbalanced datasets. Again, the better performances are obtained by applying J48 and RF algorithms. The best accuracy 80.22% is achieved with J48 algorithm using all features TF-IDF + TS + US. Classifications accuracies in references [22]–[24] are 76%, 45% and 64% respectively. Our accuracy results are 71.70 and 80.22%. Although it is difficult to compare results of different research studies that use different data sets, we obtained relatively better results than the most of other research studies.

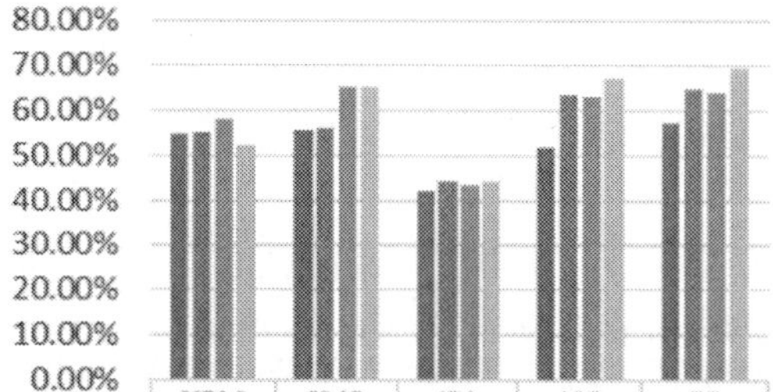

	NBM	SMO	IB1	J48	RF
TF-IDF	54.90%	55.76%	42.25%	51.61%	57.20%
TF-IDF+US	54.97%	55.86%	44.38%	63.55%	64.75%
TF-IDF+TS	57.99%	65.12%	43.31%	63.31%	64.09%
TF-IDF+US+TS	52.23%	65.33%	44.38%	67.15%	69.38%

Figure 1. Unbalanced data set experiments with 10-fold cross-validation

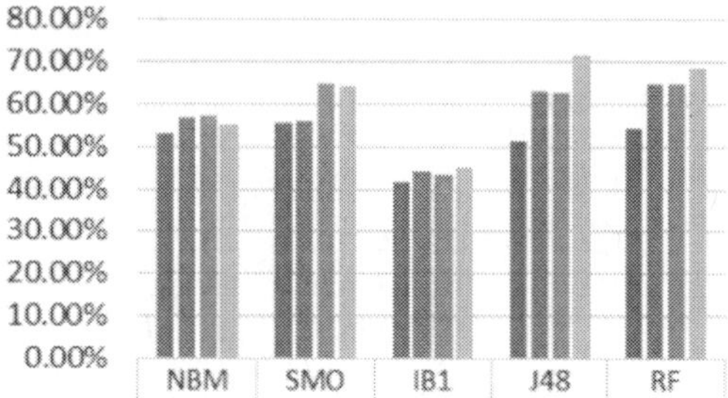

	NBM	SMO	IB1	J48	RF
TF-IDF	53.00%	55.75%	41.68%	51.46%	54.20%
TF-IDF+US	56.95%	56.09%	44.25%	63.29%	64.67%
TF-IDF+TS	57.12%	64.84%	43.40%	62.61%	65.01%
TF-IDF+US+TS	55.23%	64.32%	45.11%	71.70%	68.61%

Figure 2. Unbalanced data set experiments with repeated holdout method

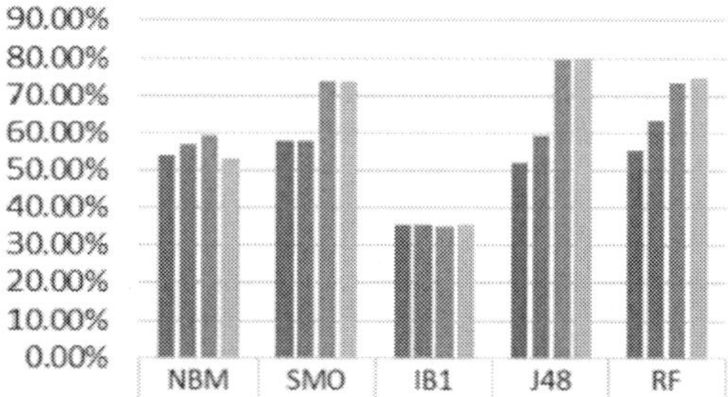

	NBM	SMO	IB1	J48	RF
TF-IDF	54.17%	57.67%	35.59%	52.18%	55.62%
TF-IDF+US	56.88%	57.67%	35.59%	59.19%	63.56%
TF-IDF+TS	59.19%	73.74%	35.25%	79.63%	73.41%
TF-IDF+US+TS	53.04%	73.88%	35.45%	80.22%	74.87%

Figure 3. Balanced data set experiments with 10-fold cross-validation

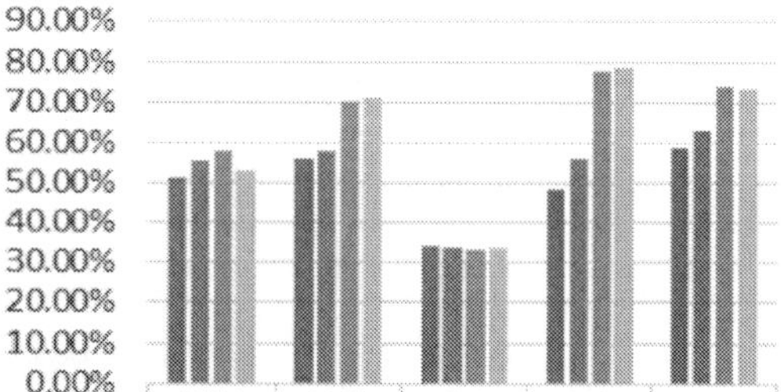

	NBM	SMO	IB1	J48	RF
TF-IDF	51.36%	56.09%	34.24%	48.42%	58.61%
TF-IDF+US	55.65%	57.98%	33.85%	56.03%	62.84%
TF-IDF+TS	57.78%	70.04%	33.27%	77.82%	73.93%
TF-IDF+US+TS	53.11%	70.82%	33.46%	78.60%	73.35%

Figure 4. Balanced data set experiments with repeated holdout

IV. CONCLUSION AND FUTURE WORK

In this study we extract additional features for Twitter sentiment classification form tweets and user information. In addition terms in a bag-of-words model weighted with TF-IDF, we also derived 8 new features about user and term usage statistics. To observe the effect of these additional features on Twitter sentiment classification we collect and label tweets and after that conduct several experiments with different conditions using several different machine learning algorithms.

Experiments show that the additional features considerably increase the performance of classifiers, especially when the dataset has a skewed class distribution. As future work, we plan to apply semi-supervised algorithms used in situations where most of the samples are unlabeled and there exists a small number of labeled samples.

REFERENCES

[1] Martin Szomszor, Patty Kostkova, and Ed De Quincey. "# swineflu: Twitter predicts swine flu outbreak in 2009." 3rd International ICST Conference on Electronic Healthcare for the 21st Century (eHEALTH2010). pp. 18-26, 2012.

[2] Jiang Bian, Umit Topaloglu, and Fan Yu. "Towards large-scale twitter mining for drug-related adverse events." Proceedings of the 2012 international workshop on Smart health and wellbeing. ACM, pp. 25-32, 2012.

[3] Le Thanh Nguyen, Pang Wu, William Chan, Wei Peng and Ying Zhang, "Predicting collective sentiment dynamics from time-series social media." Proceedings of the first international workshop on issues of sentiment discovery and opinion mining. ACM, p.6, 2012.

[4] William B. Claster, Hung Dinh, and Malcolm Cooper. "Naïve Bayes and unsupervised artificial neural nets for Cancun tourism social media data analysis." Nature and Biologically Inspired Computing (NaBIC), 2010 Second World Congress on. IEEE, pp. 158-163, 2010.

[5] Alec Go, Richa Bhayani, and Lei Huang. "Twitter sentiment classification using distant supervision." CS224N Project Report, Stanford 1.12 (2009). Mishne G., Natalie S. "Predicting Movie Sales fromBlogger Sentiment." AAAI Spring Symposium: Computational Approachesto Analyzing Weblogs. 2006.

[6] Alexander Pak, and Patrick Paroubek. "Twitter as a Corpus for Sentiment Analysis and Opinion Mining." LREc. Vol. 10. No. 2010. 2010.

[7] Dmitry Davidov, Oren Tsur, and Ari Rappoport. "Enhanced sentiment learning using twitter hashtags and smileys." Proceedings of the 23rd international conference on computational linguistics: posters. Association for Computational Linguistics, pp. 241-249, 2010.

[8] Mesut Kaya, Guven Fidan, and Ismail Hakki Toroslu. "Sentiment analysis of turkish political news." Proceedings of the The 2012 IEEE/WIC/ACM International Joint Conferences on Web Intelligence and Intelligent Agent Technology-Volume 01. IEEE Computer Society, pp. 174-180, 2012.

[9] Cumali Türkmenoglu, and Ahmet Cüneyd Tantug. "Sentiment analysis in Turkish media." Proceedings of Workshop on Issues of Sentiment Discovery and Opinion Mining, International Conference on Machine Learning (ICML), Beijing, China. 2014.

[10] Gerard Salton, and Christopher Buckley. "Term-weighting approaches in automatic text retrieval." Information processing & management 24.5 (1988): 513-523.

[11] Ian H. Witten, Eibe Frank, Mark A. Hall, and Christopher J. Pal. "Data Mining: Practical machine learning tools and techniques." Morgan Kaufmann Publishing, 2016.

[12] Ahmet Afsin Akın, and Mehmet Dündar Akın. "Zemberek, an open source NLP framework for Turkic languages." Structure 10 (2007): 1-5. 2007.

[13] PostgreSQL Relational Database, www.postgresql.org

[14] ZK Enterprise Java Web Framework, www.zkoss.org

[15] Spring Framework, www.spring.io

[16] Hibernate ORM(Object Relational Mapping), www.hibernate.org

[17] Java Programming Language, www.java.com

[18] Mingyoug Liu, and Jiangang Yang. "An improvement of TFIDF weighting in text categorization." International Proceedings of Computer Science and Information Technology (2012): 44-47.

[19] Jiawei Han, and Micheline Kamber. "Data Mining: Concepts and Techniques." Morgan Kaufmann Publishing, 2006.

[20] Pang-Ning Tan, Michael Steinbach, and Vipin Kumar. "Introduction to Data Mining." Addison-Wesley Publishing, 2006.

[21] Mehmed Kantardzic. "Data Mining: Concepts, Models, Methods, and Algorithms." John Wiley & Sons Publishing, 2003.

[22] A. Gural Vural, B. Barla Cambazoglu, Pinar Senkul, and Z. Ozge Tokgoz. "A framework for sentiment analysis in Turkish: Application to polarity detection of movie reviews in Turkish." Computer and Information Sciences III. Springer London, 2013. 437-445.

[23] Mehmet Ulvi Şimşek, and Suat Özdemir. "Analysis of the relation between Turkish twitter messages and stock market index." Application of Information and Communication Technologies (AICT), 2012 6th International Conference on. IEEE, 2012.

[24] M. Fatih Amasyalı. "Active learning for Turkish sentiment analysis." Innovations in Intelligent Systems and Applications (INISTA), 2013.

Efficient Selection of Pairwise Comparisons for Computing Top-heavy Rankings

Shenshen Liang
Technology and Information Management
University of California, Santa Cruz
Santa Cruz, California 95136
Email: sliang@soe.ucsc.edu

Luca de Alfaro
Computer Science
University of California, Santa Cruz
Santa Cruz, California 95136
Email: luca@ucsc.edu

***Abstract*—Crowdsourcing provides an efficient way to gather information from humans for solving large scale problems. Learning to rank via pairwise comparison is one of the most essential tasks in crowdsourcing, and it is widely used in applications, such as recommendation systems, online contests, player matching, and more. While much research has been done on how to aggregate the comparison data into an overall ranking, comparatively less research has been done on how to optimally select items for pairwise comparison. In this research, we consider ranking problems where the benefit for each item to be ranked in position n is a geometrically decreasing function of n. This geometric dependence between ranking and benefit is common online and on the web. We define the quality of a ranking as the total mis-allocated benefit, so that in learning a ranking, we are more sensitive to errors in the ordering of top items than errors in items ordered in the long tail. We propose and compare several active learning methods for selecting pairs for comparison. The methods actively search for the pairs to compare, present them to the crowd, and update the ranking according to the comparison outcomes. We show experimentally that the best-performing method selects pairs on the basis of the expected benefit mis-allocation between the items in the pair. As the size of the ranking problem grows, the computational cost of selecting the optimal pair for each comparison becomes prohibitive. We propose and show an efficient algorithm that selects items in batches while retains nearly optimal performance, at a cost per comparison that grows only logarithmically with the total number of items.**

Keywords–Top-heavy Ranking; Pairwise Comparison; Active Learning; Crowdsourcing.

I. Introduction

Crowdsourcing systems obtain small pieces of information from ordinary crowds and have been proven effective to get human-power information with relatively low cost [1]. They have been extensively used online, such as Wikipedia, Amazon Mechanical Turk, Quora and Stack Exchange Network.

Ranking is one of the key problems in crowdsourcing and is widely used in a variety of applications. Typically, it is performed on the basis of three types of input: binary relevance label, which categorizes data into two types such as relevant/irrelevant, true/false, etc.; graded relevance label, which classifies data into multiple ordinal levels; and pairwise preference, where a label is expressed as preference between two items rather than an absolute judgment. Each type of input is a tradeoff between potential information gain and difficulty of getting effective information. For example, for data with five star graded relevance labels, while it obtains finer-grained information than binary relevance labels, users are more prone to bias and errors. Pairwise preference, on the other hand, is a simple expression of preference between two items. Such data is relatively easy to obtain, it is less prone to errors because of its simplicity, and can be expanded to graded relevance label [2]. As a result, ranking via pairwise comparisons becomes an essential task in ranking problems.

Extensive research has been done on how to aggregate pairwise comparisons into accurate rankings, such as Mallows [3], nuclear norm minimization [4], Bradley-Terry [5], Glicko [6], TrueSkill [7] and so on [8][9]. However, it is still very challenging to efficiently obtain data with minimal computational cost. Therefore, we concentrate on studying active learning strategies for selecting pairs of items to be sent to the crowd for comparison, so that rankings will converge as quickly as possible to the correct rank. Specifically, in this paper we focus on rankings where an ordinal rank k is associated with a benefit proportional to its position. These type of geometric benefit distributions are typical in online settings, where higher rank commands geometrically higher visibility, and revenue [2][10][11].

In setting the problem, we assume that each item in a ranking has an intrinsic "quality", and we define a "top-heavy" version of ranking distance where the mis-placement of items is weighed according to $1/k^{\lambda}$ for rank k with $\lambda > 0$; this will be used to judge the speed of convergence of the proposed methods. Thus, errors in the head of the ranking will be weighed more heavily than errors in the tail. As ranking aggregation is not our primary focus, we perform ranking aggregation by applying the Glicko [6] and TrueSkill [7], which are well-established on-line aggregation algorithms.

We then formulate and compare two active learning strategies for selecting the next pairs of items to compare. In particular, we define the *loss* (or error) involved in each pair of items, and we consider and justify strategies that select pairs for comparison that have maximum loss, or that lead to maximum ranking change. We identify one such strategy, *maximum loss,* as the one that leads to overall best results, as demonstrated by our simulations.

These pair selection strategies are computationally expensive, as they require at each round the computation of many alternatives in order to select the best. To address this problem, we propose and develop efficient batched versions of the pair selection strategies, which deliver essentially the same performance while exhibiting complexity that grows only logarithmically with the number of items, the dominant step being a sorting step.

Our contributions can be summarized as follows:

- We define a distance to measure "top-heavy" rankings.
- We propose two active learning strategies for selecting pairs effectively which reduce ranking loss rapidly.
- We propose an efficient batch algorithm with low computational cost.

After a review of related work in Section II, we define the problem precisely, and describe the Glicko and TrueSkill methods for ranking aggregation (Section III). In Section IV we present our active learning methods for selecting pairs, and in Section V we present and analyze the experimental results.

II. Related Work

Obtaining data from crowdsourcing is widely applied in many fields, such as advertising, ranking, knowledge sharing, elections, opinion collection, and so on [12][13]. Many applications collect boolean or grade-based feedback about individual items. For example, StackOverFlow provides a vote up and vote down mechanism and allows users stating whether a question is useful. Yelp asks users to grade merchants in a 1 to 5 star grade-based rating system.

Much research has been done on how to aggregate comparison outcomes into a ranking [14]–[19]. Generally, ranking aggregation methods can be categorized into three types: permutation-based, such as researches in Mallows [3] and CPS [15] models; matrix factorization, such as work in [4]; and score-based probabilistic method, such as Plackett-Luce [20][21], Bradley-Terry [5], Thurstone [22], etc. Permutation methods are generally computational expensive, while matrix factorization methods do not have sufficient probabilistic interpretations. As a result, we use score-based methods for ranking aggregation in this paper.

Score-based methods assign a score to each item, and use all scores to generate rankings. Among score-based methods learning from pairwise data, the Elo ranking method is perhaps the first Bayesian pairwise ranking algorithm [23], and it is widely used in ranking sports and estimating the underlying skills of players. A player's skill is assumed to follow a Gaussian distribution with two parameters as average skill level and players uncertainty. Glickman extended Bradley-Terry model and updated player skills based on designed length of period, assuming same Gaussian distribution of player skills [6]. Trueskill by Microsoft is another Bayesian ranking system with Gaussian distribution assumption [7]. It extendes a Thurstone-Mosteller model which adds a latent variable as player performance.

Ranking aggregation via pairwise comparisons aims at computing a ranking for items that can represent all the comparison outcomes with minimum data disagreement. The problem that concerns us in this paper is how to optimally select pairs for comparison, so that a "good" ranking can be obtained with as few comparisons as possible, and thus, as efficiently as possible.

Active learning is an effective way to improve efficiency and promote performance. It has been recognized that by properly selecting items, learning tasks achieve better accuracy and require less data for training [24]–[27]. There are mainly three types of active learning methods. The first one is uncertainty sampling, which targets at finding items that the system is most uncertain about [28][29]. Another one is minimizing expected loss, which focuses on searching for items that can reduce highest expected error [30]. Lastly, query by committee method looks for items that a set of learners (refers as committee) having largest disagreement with [31][32]. While extensive research has been performed on active learning, most of them are for binary or graded based problems [33]–[39].

Some research was done on active learning for ranking from pairwise comparisons. Donmez et al. applied their document selection algorithm to RankSVM and RankBoost [40]. Also using RankSVM, Yu proposed to add most ambiguous document pairs to training dataset [41]. Chen et al. proposed a framework to find reliable annotators and informative pairs jointly, which requires annotator quality information [42]. A maximum likelihood based algorithm was proposed by Guo et al. to locate the topmost item in a ranking [43]. Other research based on pairwise comparisons includes work done by Chu et al. [44], Ailon [45], Jamieson et al. [46] and so on. Notably, a majority of them focus on selecting annotators rather than items.

III. Top-Heavy Ranking

A ranking problem consists in sorting a set of items $S = \{s_1, s_2, \ldots, s_n\}$ according to their quality. Ranking problems are solved via crowdsourcing when assessing the quality of an item requires human judgement, as is the case, for instance, when assessing the quality or appeal of videos, images or merchandise. We consider here ranking problems that are *top-heavy* in their reward: being ranked in position k has value proportional to $1/k$.

These top-heavy problems find application whenever the ranking is used to display the items to users. In such cases, a higher rank commands a larger amount of user engagement, which can be measured in item views, page visits, user votes and so forth, according to the nature of the items being ranked. As user attention is valuable (and can be monetized), we assume that the *value* of being ranked in position k is proportional to $1/k^\lambda$, for some $\lambda > 0$. We call this a λ-top heavy ranking. This is equivalent to assuming that user attention follows a Zipf distribution, an assumption that has been validated on the Web [47].

A. Ranking Quality

To measure the quality of a ranking, we introduce a measure of *distance* between top-heavy rankings. Our distance will give more weight to differences among top positions than to differences among positions in the tail of rankings. This reflects the intuition that errors in top rankings matter more than errors in the tails of rankings, as there is much more value in the top than in the tail. For instance, in a sport competition where athlete sponsorship is proportional to the inverse of the rank, it would obviously be worse to get the order wrong between the first and second positions than between the 101st and the 102nd.

Precisely, for our set of items $S = \{s_1, s_2, \ldots, s_n\}$, consider two rankings r and r' so that $r(i)$ is the position (the ordinal) of item s_i according to ranking r, for $1 \leq i \leq n$, and similarly for r'. We define the distance $d(r, r')$ between r

and r' by:

$$d(r, r') = \sum_{i=1}^{n} \left| \frac{1}{r(i)^{\lambda}} - \frac{1}{r'(i)^{\lambda}} \right| , \quad (1)$$

where λ is the coefficient of the λ-top heavy ranking. Equation (1) can be understood as follows. If r is the correct ranking, and r' is another ranking, then $|\frac{1}{r(i)^{\lambda}} - \frac{1}{r'(i)^{\lambda}}|$ is the amount of value that item i receives in error, either in positive or negative. Thus, the quantity (1) represents the total value mis-allocation of ranking r', measured with respect to ranking r.

In particular, if r^* is the correct ranking, we denote by

$$\mathcal{L}(r) = d(r, r^*) \quad (2)$$

the *loss* of r, measured as its distance from optimality.

B. Learning Top-Heavy Rankings

Our goal consists in developing algorithms for learning top-heavy rankings via crowdsourcing. The algorithms we develop follow the following scheme:

1) We start with a random ranking.
2) At each round:
   a) We select two items, and we ask a user to compare them.
   b) We use the result of the comparison to update the rankings.

We rely on binary comparisons because they are the most elementary of comparisons, and they require less cognitive load on the user than multi-way comparisons. The goal of the above process is to converge as quickly as possible to the optimal ranking according to distance (1), that is, to reduce the loss of the rank as quickly as possible. As our distance is top-weighed, this means identifying the top items early.

In this paper, we focus on step 2a: the selection of the items to be compared. Once two items are compared, there are several classical methods for updating a ranking according to the comparison outcome; we describe two such alternative methods, Glicko and Trueskill, in the following. Our focus here is on how to choose the elements whose comparison will reduce ranking loss in the fastest possible way, and with low computational cost. Intuitively, choosing the elements to compare entails estimating which elements might be incorrectly ranked, keeping into account that errors at the top matter more than errors in the tail of the ranking. As the choice of the pairs to be compared uses information from the ranking update step, we first describe the ranking update step, and subsequently our proposed methods for item selection.

C. Ranking Update Methods

We describe here two ranking update methods: Glicko [6], and TrueSkill [7].

1) Glicko: The Glicko [6] method for ranking update models each item as having a score that has a Gaussian distribution. Thus, for each item s_i, Glicko stores the median μ_i and the standard deviation σ_i of the score. The model further assumes that if two items s_i, s_j have scores X_i and X_j (sampled from their respective distributions), then the probability that a user prefers s_i to s_j is proportional to

$$\frac{e^{\kappa(X_i - X_j)}}{1 + e^{\kappa(X_i - X_j)}} ,$$

where $\kappa > 0$ is an arbitrary scaling constant. This is known as the Bradley-Terry model of match outcomes [5]. In [6], the constant is $\kappa = (\log 10)/400$, and was chosen to scale the resulting scores so that they would approximate the scores of the Elo ranking for chess players [23]. The value of the constant is immaterial to the ranking being produced (it is simply a scaling for the scores), and we choose $\kappa = 1$ in our implementation.

With these choices, once a comparison is done, the Glicko model parameters are updated as follows. Denote with s_{ij} the outcome of comparison between item s_i and item s_j:

$$s_{ij} = \begin{cases} 1 & \text{if } i \text{ wins } j \\ 0 & \text{if } j \text{ wins } i \end{cases}$$

Let also for $i = 1, 2$,

$$g(\sigma_i^2) = \frac{1}{\sqrt{1 + 3q^2\sigma^2/\pi^2}}$$

The update formulas for the mean and standard deviations are:

$$\mu_i' = \mu_i + \frac{q}{\frac{1}{\sigma_i^2} + \frac{1}{\delta_i^2}} g(\sigma_j^2)(s_{ij} - z_j)$$

$$\sigma_i'^2 = \left(\frac{1}{\sigma_i^2} + \frac{1}{\delta_i^2} \right)^{-1}$$

where

$$z_j = \frac{1}{1 + e^{-g(\sigma_j^2)(\mu - \mu_j)}}$$

$$\delta_i^2 = \left[q^2 \left(g(\sigma_j^2) \right)^2 z_j (1 - z_j) \right]^{-1} .$$

The above update formulas are obtained from [6] as the special case in which time decay of the scores does not occur. Glicko models time decay of scores, so that as players remain inactive, their score median decreases, and their score standard deviation increases, modeling increased uncertainty about their abilities. Such time dependence is appropriate in modeling tennis and chess scores, but not in modeling the quality of items in crowdsourcing batches of short temporal duration.

2) TrueSkill: The TrueSkill rating system [7] also assumes a Gaussian belief on online game players' skills. It estimates skills by constructing a factor graph, connecting players that have had a match together, and using approximate message passing. Trueskill was developed for players belonging to teams; we present here a simplified version without teams (or, more precisely, where all teams have one player only), which corresponds to the problem at hand.

The skill of player s_i, denoted as X_i, is again assumed to be Gaussian-distributed with mean μ_i and standard deviation σ_i. The performance of player i, denoted by Y_i, is also assumed to be Gaussian distributed, with mean value equal to X_i and standard deviation β, with β constant for all players. Thus, X_i models the intrinsic quality of item s_i, whereas Y_i models the actual performance of player s_i in a specific match. Translated into our setting, Y_i models how the quality of an item is perceived by the worker performing the comparison. A tie between s_i and s_j occurs when $|Y_i - Y_j| \leq \varepsilon$ for a chosen ε, while s_i is preferred to s_j when $Y_i - Y_j > \varepsilon$.

If denote $\boldsymbol{Z}$ as whole set of game outcomes, the skills of all players as $\boldsymbol{X}$, the performances of all players as $\boldsymbol{Y}$, and all differences between the performances of two players as $\boldsymbol{D}$, the general Bayesian inference problem is:

$$\begin{aligned} p(\boldsymbol{X}|\boldsymbol{Z}) &\propto \iint p(\boldsymbol{Z}, \boldsymbol{D}, \boldsymbol{Y}, \boldsymbol{X})\, d\boldsymbol{D}\, d\boldsymbol{Y} \\ &= \iint p(\boldsymbol{Z}|\boldsymbol{D}) p(\boldsymbol{D}|\boldsymbol{Y}) p(\boldsymbol{Y}|\boldsymbol{X}) p(X)\, d\boldsymbol{D}\, d\boldsymbol{Y} \end{aligned}$$

where the joint density of the entire system is presented as a product of distributions. So, the problem consists in computing a marginal probability. To solve it, Trueskill implements an approximate message passing method between nodes that correspond to the parameters of the problem. The message passing iterations stop when convergence is reached, yielding the player's skills, which correspond for us to the item qualities.

We apply TrueSkill after each comparison, updating the scores of the two items that took part in the comparison itself.

IV. Active Learning for Pair Selection

Our active learning strategies aim at selecting the pair whose comparison will reduce ranking loss most effectively. In designing pair selection strategies, we focus on strategies that select items which might be incorrectly ranked, as comparing such items is likely to be more beneficial. We propose two strategies: maximum loss and maximum ranking changes.

A. Maximum Loss

The maximum loss ranking strategy selects for comparison at each step the pair of items that have the largest expected mis-allocation of reward. To make this expected value mis-allocation precise, we define the expected loss of a pair of items as the product of the probability of the two items having incorrect relative orders by the amount of error resulting from this situation. If we denote the item with higher rank as s_i and the one with lower rank as s_j, the probability of a pair having incorrect relative orders is essentially the probability of item s_j having a larger sampled value than that of item s_i from their distributions respectively. The amount of value mis-allocation resulting from incorrect relative orders in a top-heavy ranking is $\left|\frac{1}{r(i)} - \frac{1}{r(j)}\right|$. So, our strategy of selecting maximum expected loss selects the items i, j given by:

$$\underset{(i,j)}{\arg\max} \left\{ Prob.(\tilde{s}_i < \tilde{s}_j) * \left| \frac{1}{r(i)} - \frac{1}{r(j)} \right| \right\} \tag{3}$$

where $\tilde{s}_i, \tilde{s}_j$ are sampled values from distributions of item s_i, s_j, $Prob.(\tilde{s}_i < \tilde{s}_j)$ is the probability of s_i, s_j having incorrect relative orders, and $r(i)$, $r(j)$ are the ranking positions of the items. By the properties of Gaussian distributions, the probability of $r(i)$, $r(j)$ having incorrect relative orders can be calculated as:

$$Prob.(\tilde{s}_i < \tilde{s}_j) = Prob.(\tilde{s}_i - \tilde{s}_j < 0) = \Phi\left(\frac{-|\mu_i - \mu_j|}{\sqrt{\sigma_i^2 + \sigma_j^2}} \right)$$

where μ_i, μ_j are the means and σ_i, σ_j are the standard deviations of the distributions of s_i, s_i respectively.

B. Maximum Ranking Change

The maximum ranking change strategy selects the items whose comparison is going to have the greatest impact on the current ranking. Intuitively, if two items with incorrect relative orders change their rankings after a comparison, it implies that a big problem exists potentially and the previous ranking is unstable or unreliable. In consideration of this implication, we propose a strategy selecting pairs that will get the largest expected ranking change after comparison, for items having incorrect relative rankings.

The expected ranking change for items having incorrect relative order is the product of the probability of two items having incorrect relative orders and the expected amount of change to rankings after the pair comparison. With the same notations as first strategy, and denoting the expected amount of change for items having incorrect relative order as $g(s_i \prec s_j)$, ideally we would like to select a pair of items i, j as follows:

$$\underset{(i,j)}{\arg\max} \{Prob.(\tilde{s}_i < \tilde{s}_j) * g(s_i \prec s_j)\} \tag{4}$$

where $Prob.(\tilde{s}_i < \tilde{s}_j)$ is computed as before. The expected amount of change for items having incorrect relative order can be calculated by:

$$g(s_i \prec s_j) = \left| \frac{1}{r(i)} - \frac{1}{r(i)^{s_i \prec s_j}} \right| + \left| \frac{1}{r(j)} - \frac{1}{r(j)^{s_i \prec s_j}} \right|$$

where $r(i)^{s_i \prec s_j}$ and $r(j)^{s_i \prec s_j}$ are the updated rankings of item s_i and s_i, if item s_j wins s_i in comparison.

The problem with the selection (4) is that it requires computing the outcome of all possible pair comparisons. This is very expensive computationally: in order to get the future ranking positions of the items in a pair, the algorithm has to perform quality updates for both items, and sort all items for a new ranking. To address this problem, we analyze the equation and propose an approximate version.

Equation (4) can also be expressed as:

$$\begin{aligned} & Prob.(\tilde{s}_i < \tilde{s}_j) * g(s_i \prec s_j) \qquad (5) \\ &= Prob.(\tilde{s}_i < \tilde{s}_j) * \left(\frac{1}{r(i)} - \frac{1}{r(i)^{s_i \prec s_j}} - \frac{1}{r(j)} + \frac{1}{r(j)^{s_i \prec s_j}} \right) \end{aligned}$$

Equation (5) holds because with a comparison of s_j winning s_i, the ranking update algorithms will update the ranking so that $r(j)^{s_i \prec s_j}$ ranks higher than or equivalent to $r(j)$, while $r(i)^{s_i \prec s_j}$ ranks lower than or equivalent to $r(i)$. This result is consistent with the intuition that one item shall get a lower ranking if loses, while the other shall rank higher if wins.

Assuming the ranking changes for both items are in same scale of $\alpha > 0$, i.e.,

$$\begin{cases} \frac{1}{r(i)^{s_i \prec s_j}} = \frac{1}{r(i)} * (1 + \alpha) \\ \frac{1}{r(j)^{s_i \prec s_j}} = \frac{1}{r(j)} * (1 - \alpha) \end{cases}$$

then (5) can be further expressed as:

$$\begin{aligned} & Prob.(\tilde{s}_i < \tilde{s}_j) * \left(\frac{1}{r(i)} - \frac{1}{r(i)^{s_i \prec s_j}} - \frac{1}{r(j)} + \frac{1}{r(j)^{s_i \prec s_j}} \right) \\ &= Prob.(\tilde{s}_i < \tilde{s}_j) * \left(\frac{1}{r(i)} \cdot \frac{\alpha}{(1 + \alpha)} + \frac{1}{r(j)} \cdot \frac{\alpha}{(1 - \alpha)} \right) \end{aligned} \tag{6}$$

By first order Tyler Series, while $\alpha \rightarrow 0$, $\frac{\alpha}{(1+\alpha)} \rightarrow \alpha$, $\frac{\alpha}{(1-\alpha)} \rightarrow \alpha$. Assuming $\alpha \rightarrow 0$, (6) can be approximated by:

$$Prob.(s_i \prec s_j) * \left(\frac{1}{r(i)} + \frac{1}{r(j)}\right) \cdot \alpha \tag{7}$$

$$\propto Prob.(s_i \prec s_j) * \left(\frac{1}{r(i)} + \frac{1}{r(j)}\right)$$

We assume α approaches 0 because we believe that in a ranking system with sufficient comparisons, one single comparison shall not change any item's ranking dramatically. As an example, a tennis player will not get a huge ranking drop just because he loses one game.

In light of the above approximations, the maximum ranking change strategy selects the items i, j as follows:

$$\arg\max_{(i,j)} \left\{ Prob.(s_i \prec s_j) * \left(\frac{1}{r(i)} + \frac{1}{r(j)}\right)\right\} . \tag{8}$$

Thus, the maximum ranking change pair selection strategy only relies on the current positions of items, and the computational complexity is significantly reduced.

C. Stochastic Pair Drawing

Deterministically selecting for comparison the pair with the highest value, as done in (3) and (8), carries the risk of trapping the ranking in a local optimum. To deal with this problem, we propose to use a *randomized* version of our pair selection strategies. In the randomized version, we select each pair with probability proportional to the arguments of (3) and (8), respectively. The algorithms thus still focus on the most promising pairs for comparison, but their randomized nature makes them more robust. In experiments we performed, the randomized version of the selection algorithms always outperformed the deterministic ones, so that for this paper we opted for presenting the results only for the stochastic versions, for the sake of conciseness.

D. Batch Algorithm for Efficient Selection

In many online applications, the volume of items in a ranking is huge. With such size, it is very computational expensive, or even impossible to evaluate all candidate pairs. Also, updating the ranking after every user comparison sequentially is impractical and will impose vast burden on the system. As a result, in practice, instead of sequential algorithms, batch active learning methods are widely used. Therefore, we design a batch algorithm to reduce the computational cost and make our algorithms more efficient.

In the above pair selection algorithms, we observe that items close in rank are more likely to be selected, because they have a higher probability of being incorrectly ranked. We make use of this observation in our batch algorithm to narrow the candidate pair space. For any item s_i with position $r(i)$, when selecting its candidate pairing set, we do not consider all other items: rather, the batch algorithm only looks for a subset of items immediately below s_i and evaluates the corresponding pairs. In this way, we are able to cut down evaluation pairs dramatically. Since the ranking can be incorrect, we also include in the evaluation pairs items that are sampled randomly. This randomness improves the stability of the algorithm.

Once the batch algorithm determines candidate pairing sets for all items, it uses the same active strategies to calculate values for all pairs. Then, it selects a batch of pairs stochastically, where each pair is selected with probability proportional to its value. All selected pairs are presented to users concurrently for their comparisons. After the comparison outcomes are collected, the batch algorithm updates the ranking with all outcomes at once and a new batch will be selected. In this way, the expensive process of computing pair evaluations is performed only once for every batch, rather than once for every pair presented to users.

V. EXPERIMENTS

A. Experiment Settings

We conduct experiments with simulated data as it can provide precise "true" ranking for evaluation. We assume there are 100 items, each of them has an underlying score with a Gaussian distribution, and sample its mean and variance respectively. Specifically, we sample all items' means from one Gaussian distribution as opposed to any heavy-tailed distribution, because in this paper, we focus on the intrinsic "qualities" of items that represent their strength or greatness, such as competitiveness of sports players, skills of online gamers, ratings of merchandise, reviews of restaurants; and a ranking is generated based on items' qualities. In contrast, a heavy-tailed distribution is usually assumed in relevance ranking problems, which sort items by their degree of relevance.

All pair selection strategies start with the same non-informative score estimation. Every time an algorithm requests a user comparison, we simulate it by sampling from true distributions of both items. The item with a larger sampled value is considered the winner. We conduct 20 experiments for each strategy, with 2,000 pair selections per experiment. All algorithms are evaluated with respect to the loss (2). In the experiments, we choose λ values at $0.5, 1, 2$ respectively.

B. Algorithm Loss Comparison

Figure 1 shows the loss decrease resulting from the proposed algorithms, for different λ coefficients. Along the x-axis is the number of selected pairs and along the y-axis is the average loss per experiment. The error bars indicate 95% confidence intervals, and the random strategy is used as baseline. After each pairwise comparison, the item scores are updated via Glicko and TrueSkill respectively, and a new pair to compare is selected.

The results demonstrate that our two proposed algorithms perform significantly better than the baseline. With more pairwise comparisons, it is expected to see the ranking losses of all the algorithm decreasing, but the proposed algorithms converge to the true ranking and reduce loss much faster. The 95% confidence intervals between baseline and proposed algorithms rarely overlap, illustrating that the reduction in loss resulting from our algorithms is significant. Maximum loss and maximum ranking change algorithms get comparable results at the end of experiments, with maximum loss performing slightly better. We believe it is because the approximation used in maximum ranking change introduces some loss.

Relatively, the loss decrease is slower for algorithms evaluated with a λ coefficient of 2. We believe that it is due to the top-heavy reduction effect. With $\lambda > 1$, except for the very top of the ranking, the losses from mis-ranked elements become smaller, limiting the scope for loss decrease once the top-ranked items are correctly ranked. The divergence between algorithms and evaluation measure results in the performance decrease.

C. Sequential and Batch Version Comparison

We have also experimented with the batch version of our algoritms. We start with the same non-informative score estimation. We use 10% of total items as candidate pairing set for each item, with half of them sampled from the immediately lower ranked elements, and half of them sampled randomly. The batch size is set at 20, so the ranking will be updated after collecting 20 pairwise comparisons from users.

Sharing the same x-axis and y-axis as Figure 1, Figure 2 shows loss decrease of sequential and batch versions of each algorithm. It is evident that in spite of evaluating only 10% of all pairs, the batch versions achieve almost same performances as sequential versions. The results demonstrate that the batch versions of our algorithms are capable of getting comparable performance as the sequential versions, while dramatically reducing the computational cost. Figure 3 illustrates that the average run time per experiment of the batch versions are significantly smaller than that of the sequential versions. Collectively, Figures 2 and 3 prove that our batch algorithms are an effective solution to ranking problems with large dataset.

VI. Conclusion and Future Work

In this paper, we propose two active learning strategies for selecting pairwise comparisons for top-heaving rankings, where top ranking items are considered more critical than items lower in the rankings. To address the computational challenge arising from large data volume, an efficient batch algorithm is proposed and applied. Our experimental results show that both active learning methods are effective at reducing ranking loss; overall, the maximum loss method achieves slightly better performance. We also demonstrate how our batch algorithm can achieve comparable loss decrease results while significantly reducing computational costs.

We see several directions for future work. It is interesting to explore other approximation methods for maximum ranking change strategy. Furthermore, when a ranking only aims at selecting the top-k items, without caring about their relative order, different active learning strategies may yield superior results. Finally, other pairwise comparison aggregation methods

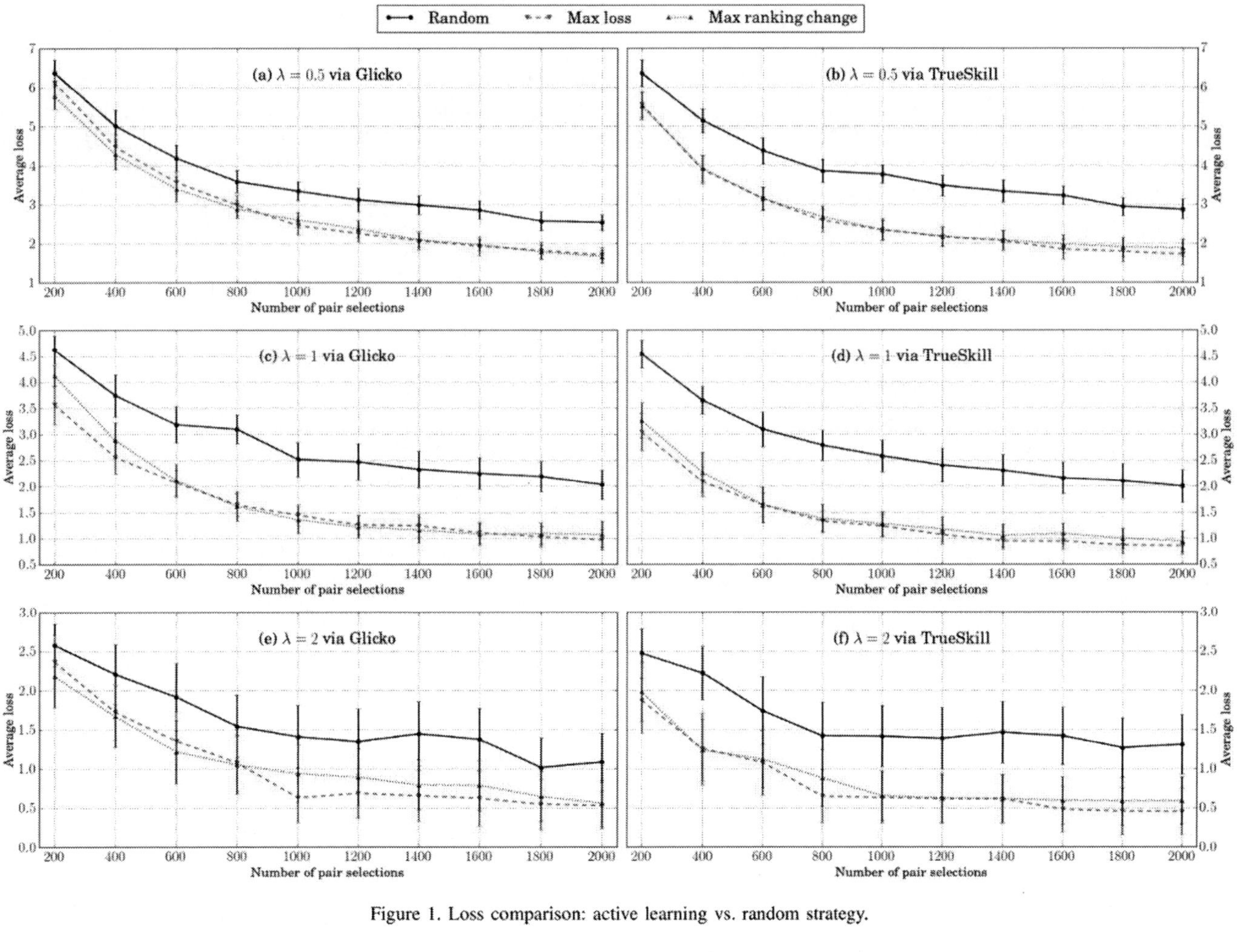

Figure 1. Loss comparison: active learning vs. random strategy.

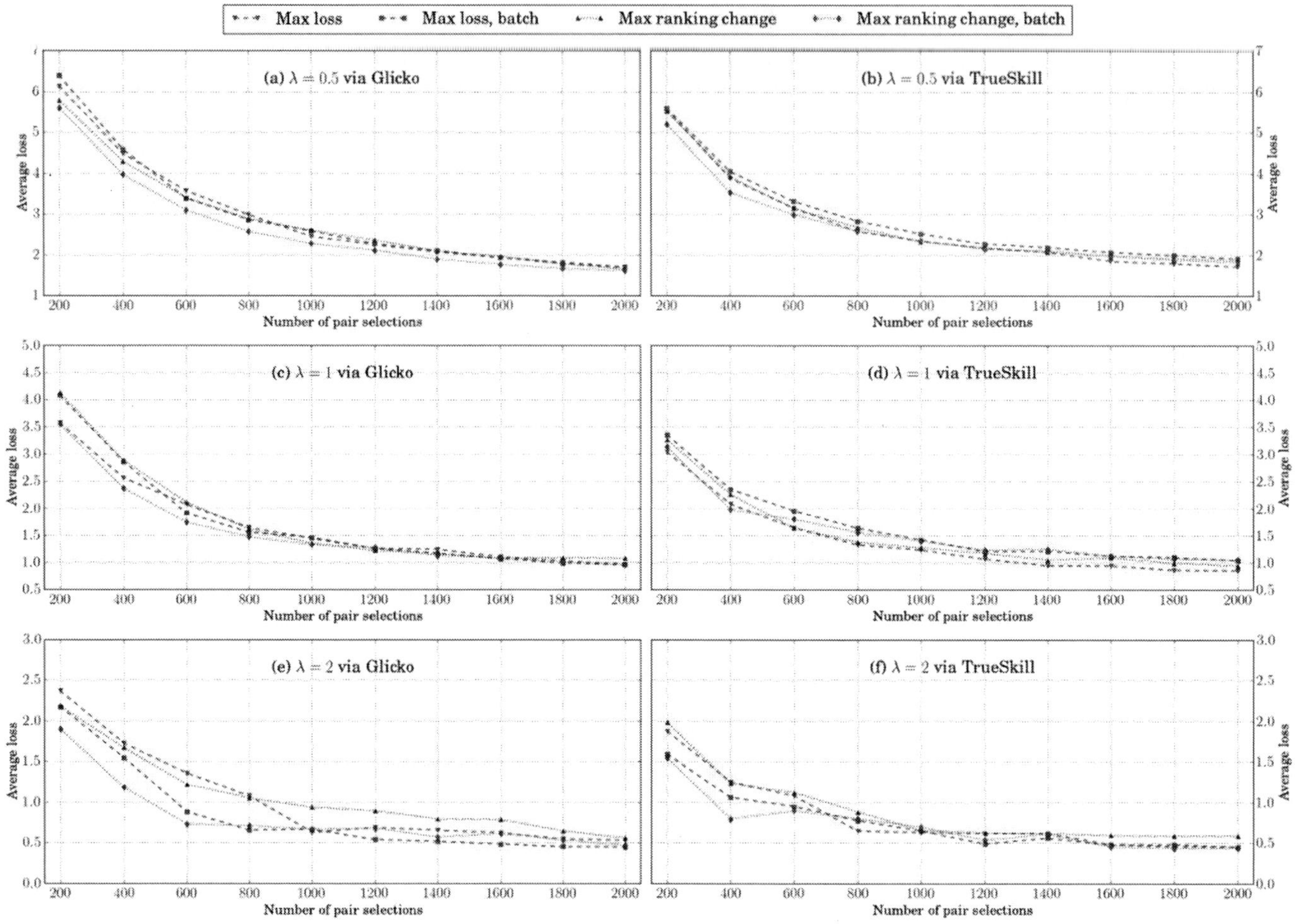

Figure 2. Loss comparison: sequential vs. batch.
The loss differences between sequential and batch versions are not significant.

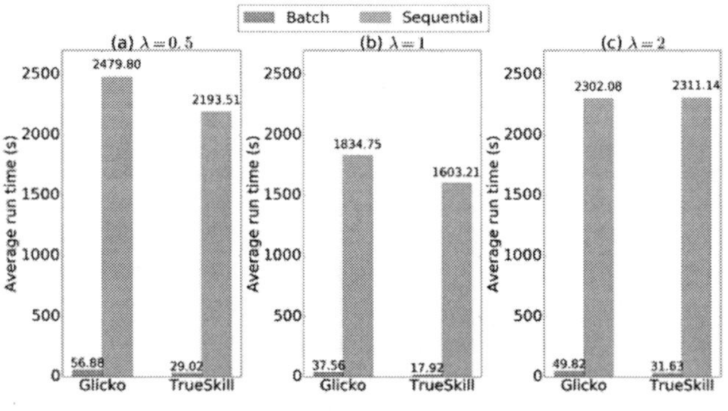

Figure 3. Average run time comparison: sequential vs. batch.

can be explored for better accuracy.

REFERENCES

[1] J. Wang, P. G. Ipeirotis, and F. Provost, "Managing crowdsourcing workers," in The 2011 winter conference on business intelligence, 2011, pp. 10–12.

[2] F. Radlinski, M. Kurup, and T. Joachims, "How does clickthrough data reflect retrieval quality?" in Proceedings of the 17th ACM Conference on Information and Knowledge Management, ser. CIKM '08. New York, NY, USA: ACM, 2008, pp. 43–52.

[3] C. L. Mallows, "Non-Null Ranking Models. I," Biometrika, vol. 44, no. 1/2, 1957, pp. 114–130.

[4] D. F. Gleich and L.-h. Lim, "Rank aggregation via nuclear norm minimization," in Proceedings of the 17th ACM SIGKDD international conference on Knowledge discovery and data mining. ACM, 2011, pp. 60–68.

[5] R. A. Bradley and M. E. Terry, "Rank analysis of Incomplete Block Designs: I. The Method of Paired Comparisons," Biometrika, vol. 39, no. 3/4, 1952, pp. 324–345.

[6] M. E. Glickman, "Parameter Estimation in Large Dynamic Paired Comparison Experiments," Journal of the Royal Statistical Society: Series C (Applied Statistics), vol. 48, no. 3, Jan. 1999, pp. 377–394.

[7] R. Herbrich, T. Minka, and T. Graepel, "TrueSkill : A Bayesian Skill Rating System," in Advances in Neural Information Processing Systems 19, B. Schlkopf, J. C. Platt, and T. Hoffman, Eds. MIT Press, 2007, pp. 569–576.

[8] D. R. Karger, S. Oh, and D. Shah, "Iterative learning for reliable crowdsourcing systems," in Advances in neural information processing systems, 2011, pp. 1953–1961.

[9] C. Burges et al., "Learning to rank using gradient descent," in Proceedings of the 22nd international conference on Machine learning. ACM, 2005, pp. 89–96.

[10] O. Chapelle, D. Metlzer, Y. Zhang, and P. Grinspan, "Expected Reciprocal Rank for Graded Relevance," in Proceedings of the 18th ACM Conference on Information and Knowledge Management, ser. CIKM '09. New York, NY, USA: ACM, 2009, pp. 621–630.

[11] G. V. Cormack, C. L. A. Clarke, and S. Buettcher, "Reciprocal Rank Fusion Outperforms Condorcet and Individual Rank Learning Methods," in Proceedings of the 32Nd International ACM SIGIR Conference on Research and Development in Information Retrieval, ser. SIGIR '09. New York, NY, USA: ACM, 2009, pp. 758–759.

[12] E. Kamar, S. Hacker, and E. Horvitz, "Combining human and machine intelligence in large-scale crowdsourcing," in Proceedings of the 11th International Conference on Autonomous Agents and Multiagent Systems-Volume 1. International Foundation for Autonomous Agents and Multiagent Systems, 2012, pp. 467–474.

[13] K. Crammer, M. Kearns, and J. Wortman, "Learning from multiple sources," The Journal of Machine Learning Research, vol. 9, 2008, pp. 1757–1774.

[14] Y. Freund, R. Iyer, R. E. Schapire, and Y. Singer, "An efficient boosting algorithm for combining preferences," The Journal of machine learning research, vol. 4, 2003, pp. 933–969.

[15] T. Qin, X. Geng, and T.-Y. Liu, "A new probabilistic model for rank aggregation," in Advances in neural information processing systems, 2010, pp. 1948–1956.

[16] T.-K. Huang, R. C. Weng, and C.-J. Lin, "Generalized bradley-terry models and multi-class probability estimates," The Journal of Machine Learning Research, vol. 7, 2006, pp. 85–115.

[17] P. Smyth, U. Fayyad, M. Burl, P. Perona, and P. Baldi, "Inferring Ground Truth from Subjective Labelling of Venus Images," in Advances in Neural Information Processing Systems 7, G. Tesauro, D. S. Touretzky, and T. K. Leen, Eds. Cambridge, MA: The MIT Press, 1995, pp. 1085–1092.

[18] F. Wauthier, M. Jordan, and N. Jojic, "Efficient Ranking from Pairwise Comparisons," in PMLR, Feb. 2013, pp. 109–117.

[19] S. Negahban, S. Oh, and D. Shah, "Iterative Ranking from Pair-wise Comparisons," in Proceedings of the 25th International Conference on Neural Information Processing Systems, ser. NIPS'12. USA: Curran Associates Inc., 2012, pp. 2474–2482.

[20] R. D. Luce, Individual choice behavior: A theoretical analysis. Courier Corporation, 2005.

[21] R. L. Plackett, "The analysis of permutations," Applied Statistics, 1975, pp. 193–202.

[22] L. L. Thurstone, "The method of paired comparisons for social values." The Journal of Abnormal and Social Psychology, vol. 21, no. 4, 1927, p. 384.

[23] A. E. Elo, The rating of chess players, past and present. Arco Pub., 1978.

[24] P. Donmez and J. G. Carbonell, "Active sampling for rank learning via optimizing the area under the ROC curve," in Advances in Information Retrieval. Springer, 2009, pp. 78–89.

[25] F. Radlinski and T. Joachims, "Active exploration for learning rankings from clickthrough data," in Proceedings of the 13th ACM SIGKDD international conference on Knowledge discovery and data mining. ACM, 2007, pp. 570–579.

[26] D. A. Cohn, Z. Ghahramani, and M. I. Jordan, "Active learning with statistical models," Journal of artificial intelligence research, 1996.

[27] B. Long et al., "Active learning for ranking through expected loss optimization," in Proceedings of the 33rd international ACM SIGIR conference on Research and development in information retrieval. ACM, 2010, pp. 267–274.

[28] S. Tong and D. Koller, "Support vector machine active learning with applications to text classification," The Journal of Machine Learning Research, vol. 2, 2002, pp. 45–66.

[29] D. J. C. MacKay, "Information-Based Objective Functions for Active Data Selection," Neural Computation, vol. 4, no. 4, Jul. 1992, pp. 590–604.

[30] N. Roy and A. McCallum, "Toward optimal active learning through monte carlo estimation of error reduction," ICML, Williamstown, 2001, pp. 441–448.

[31] P. Melville and R. J. Mooney, "Diverse ensembles for active learning," in Proceedings of the twenty-first international conference on Machine learning. ACM, 2004, p. 74.

[32] Y. Freund, H. S. Seung, E. Shamir, and N. Tishby, "Selective sampling using the query by committee algorithm," Machine learning, vol. 28, no. 2-3, 1997, pp. 133–168.

[33] M. Fang, J. Yin, and D. Tao, "Active learning for crowdsourcing using knowledge transfer." in AAAI, 2014, pp. 1809–1815.

[34] Y. Yan, G. M. Fung, R. Rosales, and J. G. Dy, "Active learning from crowds," in Proceedings of the 28th international conference on machine learning (ICML-11), 2011, pp. 1161–1168.

[35] F. Laws, C. Scheible, and H. Schtze, "Active learning with amazon mechanical turk," in Proceedings of the conference on empirical methods in natural language processing. Association for Computational Linguistics, 2011, pp. 1546–1556.

[36] J. Costa, C. Silva, M. Antunes, and B. Ribeiro, "On using crowdsourcing and active learning to improve classification performance," in Intelligent Systems Design and Applications (ISDA), 2011 11th International Conference on. IEEE, 2011, pp. 469–474.

[37] P. Donmez and J. G. Carbonell, "Proactive learning: cost-sensitive active learning with multiple imperfect oracles," in Proceedings of the 17th ACM conference on Information and knowledge management. ACM, 2008, pp. 619–628.

[38] U. Paquet et al., "Vuvuzelas & Active Learning for Online Classification," in NIPS Workshop on Comp. Social Science and the Wisdom of Crowds, 2010.

[39] C. Campbell, N. Cristianini, A. Smola, and others, "Query learning with large margin classifiers," in ICML, 2000, pp. 111–118.

[40] P. Donmez and J. G. Carbonell, "Optimizing Estimated Loss Reduction for Active Sampling in Rank Learning," in Proceedings of the 25th International Conference on Machine Learning, ser. ICML '08. New York, NY, USA: ACM, 2008, pp. 248–255.

[41] H. Yu, "SVM selective sampling for ranking with application to data retrieval," in Proceedings of the eleventh ACM SIGKDD international conference on Knowledge discovery in data mining. ACM, 2005, pp. 354–363.

[42] X. Chen, P. N. Bennett, K. Collins-Thompson, and E. Horvitz, "Pairwise ranking aggregation in a crowdsourced setting," in Proceedings of the sixth ACM international conference on Web search and data mining. ACM, 2013, pp. 193–202.

[43] S. Guo, A. Parameswaran, and H. Garcia-Molina, "So Who Won?: Dynamic Max Discovery with the Crowd," in Proceedings of the 2012 ACM SIGMOD International Conference on Management of Data, ser. SIGMOD '12. New York, NY, USA: ACM, 2012, pp. 385–396.

[44] W. Chu and Z. Ghahramani, "Extensions of gaussian processes for ranking: semisupervised and active learning," in Proceedings of the NIPS 2005 Workshop on Learning to Rank. MIT, 2005, pp. 29–34.

[45] N. Ailon, "An Active Learning Algorithm for Ranking from Pairwise Preferences with an Almost Optimal Query Complexity," J. Mach. Learn. Res., vol. 13, no. 1, Jan. 2012, pp. 137–164.

[46] K. G. Jamieson and R. D. Nowak, "Active Ranking Using Pairwise Comparisons," in Proceedings of the 24th International Conference on Neural Information Processing Systems, ser. NIPS'11. USA: Curran Associates Inc., 2011, pp. 2240–2248.

[47] B. A. Huberman, P. L. T. Pirolli, J. E. Pitkow, and R. M. Lukose, "Strong Regularities in World Wide Web Surfing," Science, vol. 280, no. 5360, Apr. 1998, pp. 95–97.

AUTHOR INDEX